Profit Wise

How to Make More Money in Business by
Doing the Right Thing

Jeff Morrill

TCK PUBLISHING.COM

Published by TCK Publishing
www.TCKpublishing.com

Get discounts and special deals on our best-selling books at
www.TCKpublishing.com/bookdeals

To Julie, my wife and highest value-added stakeholder.
Who said a business book couldn't be romantic?

Table of Contents

Introduction

I'm going to show you how to grow a more profitable company by doing the right thing. Along the way, you'll discover hundreds of actionable business insights. I developed most of these breakthrough business techniques the hard way.

I founded my first business, Planet Subaru, from scratch and with very little money. I acquired most of my professional education building that company into one of the most successful privately-owned automotive dealerships in the United States. I later created and still own businesses that yield over $100 million in annual revenue in markets that include insurance, real estate, and cell tower infrastructure. I've also collected lessons along the way by reading lots of books, observing smart people, and learning from mentors and advisors over my last quarter century in business.

You'll hear about some things I discovered on the showroom floor, but this isn't a book about the automotive industry—it's about how you can build a better business and a better world at the same time. With a little inspiration and a lot of effort, your thriving company can produce great value with great values.

Not every idea will be new to you, and some may not speak to you at this time in your life. But I promise you this: at least one story, suggestion, technique, or perspective shared in this book will shift your thinking in a significant way, and that one evolution will pay back your investment in the book many times over. You'll also find dozens of valuable insights that you can apply immediately to improve your business, have more fun, and serve others.

I didn't write this book to make money or sell anything; in fact, I'm donating all my royalties to charity. I wrote it because I want to show you how to make more money over the long term and enjoy yourself along the way by focusing your whole company on doing the right thing. You really can outsell your competitors without selling out your integrity. I will help you become more profit wise and your business more profit able.

This is the book I wish I had read earlier in life to help me bypass some of the painful and expensive mistakes I made while struggling to achieve success in business. A Chinese proverb says that the best time to plant a tree is twenty years ago, but the second-best time is now. I can't send this book back in time to my younger self, but I can do the next best thing, which is sharing that knowledge with you today.

Here are some of the things you'll learn:

In Chapter 1, you'll unravel the paradox of making more money by focusing less on the bottom line. Putting a few key priorities ahead of this month's financial statement will make you far richer, both financially and spiritually.

In Chapter 2, you'll discover what makes your business special and acquire the techniques to rally your team around those core values. People accomplish consequential achievements when they work well together and share a common purpose. Your most important role as a leader is to define reality for your coworkers, customers, and community.

In Chapter 3, you'll learn how to recruit peak performers who share your values and achieve superior results. You can start using our straightforward hiring process immediately. You'll know exactly which questions to ask during interviews, how to expand and improve your pool of candidates, and how to select the best people for the job.

In Chapter 4, you'll learn how to improve your leadership skills and create durable trust among your team. You'll develop a healthy culture and provide your workforce with everything they need to be passionate and productive.

In Chapter 5, you'll uncover various ways to deliver your marketing messages to likely customers, and learn our techniques for reaching new buyers for free by enlisting the media and your existing customers to share your business's story.

In Chapter 6, you'll learn to serve customers more effectively when they show up at your business, so they buy today and enjoy the experience enough to come back again.

In Chapter 7, you'll discover how to improve your negotiating skills—not by taking advantage of people, but by making sure everybody gets a fair shake. You'll find practical tips for getting more of what you want.

In Chapter 8, you'll learn how to make better, faster decisions and evaluate your mistakes so you don't make them twice.

In Chapter 9, you'll discover systems to make the highest and best use of your time at work and leave enough battery power for the other responsibilities and joys in your life. You'll spend your time more intentionally on the things that matter most. You'll make better use of your days so you can make the most of your life.

In Chapter 10, you'll learn a simple process for closing the gap between your current self and the person you really want to be. And because temporary or permanent burnout affects most entrepreneurs, I'll show you how to avoid it, or at least prepare for it, so you and your business are ready when you need to scale back.

Online Resources

And there's more! I have so many useful business tools for you that the publisher couldn't fit all of them in the book:

- Bonus chapters on starting a business, including:
  - ➤ Crucial questions to ask yourself before launching;
  - ➤ How to choose the right business for you;
  - ➤ Why you need a business plan and how to get started;

- Diagnostic worksheets for improving your business;
- The exact checklists, templates, and other process documents described in the book that we use every day in our companies (and you should too).

You can enjoy unlimited free access to all these resources at jeffmorrill.com/reader-tools.

CHAPTER 1

Take the High Road to Raise the Bottom Line

Author E.L. Doctorow said of driving in fog at night, "You can only see as far as your headlights, but you can make the whole trip that way." He was referring to the art of beginning a novel, but his keen observation also applies to business and life: you can't prepare for every possible eventuality at the beginning of a project. For most things, you just have to get started and figure it out as you go.

My brother and I opened our first company, Planet Subaru, in Massachusetts on October 2, 1998. John was thirty-two and I was twenty-six. We did not begin with any financial wealth, inherited or otherwise. We had some modest savings, and we borrowed a few hundred thousand dollars to purchase and capitalize the business. Then we borrowed a few million more to pay for all the cars. We were perilously leveraged, so we needed to achieve profitability immediately. The predecessor dealership, Norwell Subaru, had opened in April, went bankrupt in August, and lost a half million dollars in between.

As a little kid, John had always wanted to be in the car business, and sure enough, he had wound up working at Ford Motor Company in Detroit. I ended up in the car business by accident. I was interested in public service, so during college I had interned with the lieutenant governor in Virginia, where we had grown up. When I graduated in 1994, he didn't have any openings on his small office staff, but he offered me a job in the service department of his business, Don Beyer Volvo.

During the years we spent working for others, John and I discussed a dream to open our own business that would offer an alternative experience to the high-pressure sales tactics and questionable ethics of the typical dealership. I started calling people who were advertising dealerships for sale in the classified section of Automotive News. After plenty of dead ends and false starts, I found a couple of guys who had crashed their Subaru store in Norwell, Massachusetts, and needed to sell it quickly. Nine weeks later, Planet Subaru sold its first car, a brand-new 1999 Outback, to a retired couple from Hingham. We sold thirty-four new cars and six used cars that month. (Nowadays we sell hundreds every month.) We worked seven long days a week and posted a tiny net profit of $713, a herculean accomplishment for a first month in business.

Ever since that first month, we've been taking the high road to raise the bottom line. I'll explain it all in detail later, but here are just a few examples of how we do that:

Even today, car dealerships and many other employers hire the same sort of person, disregarding those who don't fit a particular profile. We seek applicants that other dealerships generally don't recruit. For example, the very first salesperson we hired was a woman, even though women in dealerships were rare, and continue to be so today. She had no experience, but would quickly become our highest performer. We recruited another excellent salesperson after he was fired by another company when they found out he was gay. (This was legal at the time.) We quickly acquired overlooked talent by seeking people who were not well represented in the industry.

Way back in 2011, we installed a massive solar array on our roof that would power our entire showroom and reduce our carbon footprint. It cost a fortune at the time, but the system has since paid for itself in savings, and we'll enjoy free power for decades to come. Plus, the project continues to increase our revenue by attracting impressed customers from all over.

We donated a vehicle to our local river protection organization and covered it in Planet graphics. It's a rolling billboard that communicates our commitment to clean water. We support organizations doing good work in the community, and their members support us with their purchases.

Some people tell me that we're naïve to invest so many resources in expanding the diversity of our workforce, focusing on environmental stewardship, and supporting local non-profits. They say we should focus on net worth rather than planet worth. But they haven't seen our financial statements! I believe our unusual approach makes us *more* profitable, not less. We have a stronger workforce because we invest extra energy and time in recruiting diverse candidates. We spend less on utilities and facility maintenance because of our numerous environmental upgrades. And every day, customers drive past other dealerships to do business with us because we share their values.

It gets even better: we actually make more money by charging our customers less! Like most businesses, we depend on long-term relationships because the cost to acquire a new customer is much larger than the cost of satisfying a repeat customer. We organize our processes and pricing around creating customers for life. For example, we sell almost all of our new cars at a deep discount, without a customer even asking. We make less on each transaction, but our customers trust us to give them competitive prices without the headaches of shopping around. Our annual sales volume continues to increase every year, so our profits continue to grow.

Perhaps you're skeptical and think all this sounds too good to be true. I'll address some common questions I hear when sharing these ideas with other business owners and managers.

What about all the people who get rich by thinking about no one but themselves? Unfortunately, some businesspeople exploit others. They make money looking for the quickest buck, without regard to the collateral damage. They privatize all the benefits in a transaction for their own benefit, and outsource the costs to everybody else. For example, some private equity firms break up established companies, fire hundreds or thousands of people, and walk away before all the leverage causes bankruptcy. These dog-eat-dog business strategies often devastate entire communities. But even if this approach works (and it doesn't always), I argue that these bright people could have made even more money growing the long-term value in companies instead of blowing them apart. And if society needs to lose in order for you to win, the price of your financial wealth is moral poverty. Just because something might be legal doesn't necessarily mean it's right or smart. In the short term, you can often get away with anything. In the long term, what goes around has a way of coming around. You will reap the harvest of whatever seeds you spend your life planting, so choose them carefully.

If an entrepreneur spends so much time and energy focused on other stakeholders, who takes care of the stockholder? I'm not suggesting that you operate your company as a charity; it's Planet's consistent profitability that powers our community investments. You can lose money or go bankrupt if you fail to successfully execute all the fundamentals of running a business, including expense control, cash management, legal compliance, and many others. What I'm recommending is that you design your business practices so stockholders and stakeholders succeed together. For example, expanding your hiring pool to include members of underrepresented groups improves your workforce, gives those team members a good income and career path, and supports the overall economic health of your community. Win, win, win.

With so much emphasis on doing the right thing, who defends the business from predatory people? I was always the skinny kid, and I did not appreciate being bullied, so that meant I got drawn into fights. And unfortunately, I would later find that the business world isn't a whole lot different than the school yard. You will encounter people who will intentionally or unintentionally try to screw you over. I do a better job swimming around these sharks than I used to, but I still need to guard our businesses from people who would try to harm or cheat us. Just because you're committed to doing the right thing in business doesn't mean you have to let others take advantage of you. Sometimes you need to make tough decisions so you can preserve your business to serve all the people who depend on it today and into the future.

When comparing our financial results to those of our competitors, I can confidently say that we have a more profitable business model, despite the naysayers. But what if I'm wrong, and we don't produce the absolute highest possible profits? What if all I can say I did with my career was create great jobs for overlooked people, improve the community where I live, and still earn an abundant living? That sounds like a pretty good life to me.

Perhaps these ideas seem counterintuitive, but they're hardly radical. Think about other paradoxes in life: you get more love by giving more, you get luckier by working harder, and you get happier by worrying less about your own needs. Likewise, the best way to grow profits over the long run is not to obsess narrowly on this month's profits, but create enough value for other people so they want to do business with you instead of somebody else.

While building that value, you need to consider the other impacts of your actions on the world. In economics, externalities are the costs or benefits of a transaction that affect other parties. Externalities can be positive, negative, or both at once. When you drive across town to recycle your aluminum cans, you reduce landfill usage, but running your vehicle also releases harmful emissions into the atmosphere. None of us live in a vacuum; almost everything we do generates externalities, many of them negative.

When we focus exclusively on our own wealth without regard to the collateral effects, we can damage the ecological and social systems that we depend on to produce profits in the first place. Collectively, we face a staggering array of problems that threaten our very survival as a species. To name just a few, our carbon pollution causes rapid global warming, our exploitation of animals spreads deadly pathogens, and our economy destabilizes governments by creating a growing wealth gap. We have a moral obligation to run our businesses in a way that minimizes negative externalities and increases benefits to society.

Perhaps you are doing well, but that doesn't mean the world is functioning morally or sustainably. Would you be satisfied with a society that allowed 20 percent of its children to live in poverty (as we do today in the United States) if *your* child had a one-in-five chance of growing up poor and disadvantaged? Philosopher John Rawls described just this sort of question in his book, *A Theory of Justice*. If you were to build a society from scratch and make all new rules, would you create a system with so many deprived people if you might become one of them? He suggested we look past our own favorable circumstances by using a "veil of ignorance" to forget our existing station. It's like the technique your mom suggested for sharing a candy bar with a sibling—one person cuts and the other gets to pick the piece, encouraging the first to slice fairly. And when we step outside the bubble of our own good fortune, we see how urgently we need to improve everyone else's access to the same quality of life that we enjoy. You can make decisions in your business that contribute to building a just, sustainable society.

Historically, "robber barons" such as Cornelius Vanderbilt and Andrew Carnegie earned their wealth in unsavory ways, and then gave it away philanthropically at the end of their lives. Wouldn't you prefer to run your business and your life so the world might benefit all along, instead of after you're retired or dead? You can serve others as you go, so you don't need to clean up your damage later. Consider these words from the Book of Ecclesiastes in the Bible: "I know that there is nothing better for people than to be happy and to do good while they live." As an entrepreneur, you don't have to wait until the end of your days to make a difference. You can improve the world today by the way you choose to do business. You will enjoy more abundance, better relationships, and a more meaningful life, too.

Throughout the book, I will conclude each chapter with Profit Wise Questions that encourage you to discover your own insights about these topics.

Profit Wise Questions

- Would you be as successful as you are today if you had been born into an impoverished family?

- Does your company engage in any business practices that make you uncomfortable? If so, can you change them entirely, or somehow mitigate the negative effects?

- Who are the key stakeholders in your business? Are you satisfied with the way you balance their needs?

- Do you effectively communicate to various audiences all the honorable things your company does so that you might benefit from their appreciation?

CHAPTER 2

Defining Reality

Former Herman Miller CEO Max De Pree said that the most important job of a leader is to define reality. Defining reality is telling the story of why your company exists, *what* you try to accomplish, *how* you go about doing it, and *who* does the work. Your reality organizes the values and mission of your organization into a coherent story. It is even more important than your business strategy because it shapes every decision you make, including the business strategy itself.

Humans are social creatures, and we take big leaps only when we coordinate our efforts. Pick any significant achievement, such as curing polio, putting a human on the moon, or climbing Mt. Everest. The household names we associate with these successes all stood on the shoulders of large teams. They also depended upon the accumulated advancements of their societies. Jonas Salk developed the polio vaccine with knowledge discovered by previous generations of experts working in virology. Neil Armstrong hit the moon on a spear tip of unimaginable complexity, requiring vast amounts of collective expertise in math, engineering, and aeronautics. Even Norgay and Hillary's relatively compact expedition to the summit of Everest relied on prior refinements in clothing, equipment, and meteorology.

The stories we tell ourselves influence our culture and behavior. Consider paper money, made of nearly worthless material. It's only valuable because we've all agreed that it's a proxy for actual wealth. Poet Ralph Hodgson said, "Some things have to be believed to be seen." Our shared beliefs can turn lead into gold. What is the "United States of America" but an agreement that certain people living in a certain territory constitute a nation? And what is a nation but a belief among people in some common set of values, language, laws, and history? Mutual understandings allow people to band together and assemble into a force much more powerful than isolated individuals. For a fascinating investigation of these narrative forces that create and shape society, I recommend Yuval Noah Harari's book, *Sapiens*.

Your business will enjoy many benefits with a clearly defined reality. For one, it simplifies decision-making. We have a standard that our advertising will always be up front, with full disclosures on anything that might be confusing. This makes it pretty easy for any of our managers to develop and publish an advertisement without the need for bureaucratic procedures or department meetings. When we have a customer service dilemma, we consult our rule that we always do *at least* the right thing. If all your team members understand that guideline, they rarely need much coaching to help a customer. When created from healthy values, a clearly defined reality helps everyone on the team make better decisions in less time, with fewer mistakes.

At Planet, we summarize our reality in one word: *un*dealership. We are the friendly, ethical, professional alternative to the typical dealership experience.

Answer these questions to help you develop the reality for your business:

What's special about your company? Ask your customers and team members why they like working with you.

Can your reality rewrite your industry's rules in your favor? For example, dealerships have traditionally competed on price, jerking their customers around with bait-and-switch dishonesty. With our *un*dealership approach, we force our competitors into a broader conversation about values, where we compare very favorably. It is very difficult to beat a team at its own game. From Sun Tzu's *Art of War*: "To subdue the enemy without fighting is the acme of skill."

What are your company values? Is your business just about profit, or do you have additional aspirations? In our case, my brother and I decided early on that a life limited to moving iron and making money would not be enough for us. We envisioned using the abundance produced by the business in service of higher ideals. For example, we wanted to reinvest in the community by sustaining local non-profits and environmental initiatives. That mission helped us stay motivated during our early struggles, and it continues to energize our team members who share these beliefs.

What kind of people do you hire? We seek our sales professionals from outside the car business so we don't import any bad habits. We hire ambitious people who have traditionally been excluded from job opportunities in the car business.

What kind of customers do you want to attract? For example, do you prefer a price-conscious model like Costco, an exceptional customer service approach like Nordstrom, or a values strategy like Patagonia?

What are the things you won't do? For example, we make our prices and offers as transparent as possible. While this may not be radical in some industries, it's the exception in the retail car business. Among other unsavory practices, we don't use asterisks and tricky fine print. A customer should be able to walk in with a printout of our offer and pay exactly what they expect to pay.

Once you've grasped the essence of what your organization is all about (and what's it not, because you can't be all things to all people), you need to share this story with your team and bake it into your culture. Summarize your vision in some kind of simple document that can live as a tagline, mission statement, or some other kind of presentation of principles. Include this summary in your employment ads and use language that attracts the kind of people you really want working in your company. We like to recruit people who already believe in the Planet philosophy of friendly customer service and environmental responsibility. If your hires already subscribe to your values before they join the team, you'll invest less effort integrating them into your culture. Team members who understand the "why" of the organization have a much easier time with the "how."

Espousing values is much easier than living them, and I can remember a few incidents where I'm embarrassed to report that we lost sight of our *un*dealership north star. One example involved a business manager (the person who arranges car loans and sells warranties). Early on, before we were well established in the community, we struggled to attract quality applicants. Desperate to fill an open position, we hired a brusque woman who had worked at many other dealerships. She pushed people to buy products instead of selling them on their merits. She did not graciously accept a "no" when customers declined. We never should have hired her, and we waited too long to part ways. Even years later, repeat customers occasionally asked me with a hopeful tone if she had moved on. Ouch. Every little and big decision you make is either a deposit or a withdrawal in the integrity of your organization's reality.

Your work in defining reality is never done. The ancient Greek philosopher Heraclitus said, "A man never steps into the same river twice, for it's not the same river and he is not the same man." You grow, as does your organization. You need to adapt your reality to changing circumstances and continually earn the team's confidence in your reality.

Profit Wise Questions

- In one sentence or a few, what is your company's reality?
- If I asked each of your team members about that reality, what would they say?
- Is there a gap between your current and desired realities?
- Can you make changes to close that gap?
- How can you better communicate your reality internally and externally?

Online Resources

This book comes with a worksheet to help you discover and communicate your company's reality. Find it at jeffmorrill.com/reader-tools.

CHAPTER 3

Hiring

Five team members who opened the dealership in 1998 are still with us, and we kissed an army of frogs along the way to develop the rest of the award-winning workforce we have today. We can (and do) exchange *individuals* when we must, but it would require another two decades to replace our *team*. If necessary, we could replenish a depleted inventory or even buy another facility relatively quickly, but we could not write a check in any amount that would replicate our team's knowledge, skills, personal customer relationships, or ability to work together. That's why I consider the attraction and retention of the Planet team as my life's greatest professional accomplishment.

After defining reality, hiring is the most important thing you do as a leader. If you can't gather enough people with the inclination and ability to do what you ask them to do, then you run a day care facility instead of a business. Managers accomplish their goals through their teams. All the activities associated with hiring are not an interruption from the day-to-day business operations. They're the reason you come to work! Proper hiring consumes time, but the up-front investment compares favorably to the punishing costs of hiring the wrong person. And you might as well develop a good process now, because you will hire perpetually as long as you own or manage the business. For example, with our current team of over a hundred, even if all of our people stay with us for ten years each, we'll have to hire ten people per year just to replace those who leave or retire. Add in some growth, and we often need to recruit, hire, and train several people every month.

Seek Diversity to Build the Strongest Team

Few people disagree that a diverse workforce gives opportunities to individuals who might have otherwise been shut out of good jobs, and that economic mobility contributes to a healthier society. But too many owners and managers neglect to hire a diverse team because they don't see all the benefits to their own companies. They end up missing out on rare talent. Here are some of the rewards we've enjoyed by hiring people from groups traditionally excluded from the jobs in our industry (such as women, people of color, and the LGBQT community).

We dramatically expand the size of our recruiting pool in an era when competition for top performers is fierce. For example, if you're in an industry where women don't make up a sizeable percentage of the workforce, you're missing out on half of the population!

These hires tend to be more grateful, motivated, and loyal because we offered them an opportunity they couldn't find anywhere else.

We differentiate ourselves from the competition. Some customers appreciate working with team members who are like them.

We draw customers from a wider range of communities. Team members with foreign language skills, for instance, give us the ability to communicate in a customer's first language.

We make better decisions because we have more unique perspectives represented at the table. For example, we've evolved our sales process to accommodate the more or less aggressive purchasing styles common in different sub-cultures.

You'll need to invest more effort to recruit people from different backgrounds, but your customers, coworkers, community, and corporation will all enjoy the benefits.

Tips for Hiring Well

Communicate to job seekers what makes your company special. We see the greatest loyalty among our team members who share our *un*dealership values before they join us. They know we're a for-profit company, but they want to be part of our environmental initiatives, best-workplace awards, customer service philosophy, and community reinvestment efforts. We highlight these Planet differentiators in our ads and on our careers webpage. Especially during periods of low unemployment, talented people looking for jobs have other options, and you need to sell them on your special opportunity. If you just opened and can't sell a track record of success, share other benefits of working at your company, such as the excitement of joining a new venture, or the chance to get in on the ground floor and grow with the business.

Select candidates based on good character first and foremost. Character flaws can appear as thievery, narcissism, bigotry, greed, arrogance, or in other forms. People with these liabilities can poison your team spirit and draw your organization into legal and financial peril. Be vigilant about keeping them out, and fix your mistake quickly if you let one in. Character can be hard to evaluate directly, so we look for conscientious people. Conscientiousness is an excellent proxy for character, because people with the desire and ability to honor their responsibilities will rise to the occasion and rarely let you down.

Obtain extraordinary results from people who appear to be ordinary. We look to hire good people who haven't yet found the opportunity or confidence to thrive. In the right circumstances, some of these previously undistinguished candidates become standout team members. For example, we have a technician who struggled in public school, but he can disassemble a complicated engine and put it back together from memory. I still joke with him when he wraps up a job: "Where are you hiding the parts you forgot to put back on?" Every component and bolt is in the right place, and so is he. He's just a "regular" blue-collar guy, but he repairs vehicles with unusual quality and efficiency, earning his family—and ours—a great living.

Hire people who are better than you whenever possible. If you're always the smartest person in the room, you might be a genius. More likely, though, you don't have the self-confidence or the ability to recruit the best talent. And even if you *are* a genius, you're not good at everything. Savvy hiring compensates for the talents, skills, and strengths you don't have.

It's never the right time to hire the wrong person. No matter how desperate you feel, don't hire a sub-par candidate just because you need the body. We call such mistakes "mis-hires," and just like misfired bullets, they're potentially lethal. As painful as it is to operate short-handed, the costs of hiring unqualified, untrainable people are even worse.

It's never the wrong time to hire the right person. Sometimes a perfect candidate shows up when you don't have an opening, or sometimes you have two candidates you really like for only one opening. Finding an outstanding candidate consumes significant institutional resources, and there's no guarantee that you'll find someone as good the next time you need to hire. Before you discard quality candidates because of timing, bend over backwards to see if you can find a home for them somewhere in your business.

Hire the right person even if they have no experience. Many jobs are straightforward enough that the right people can learn the fundamentals and start contributing quickly, even if they've never done the job before. You can't change someone's character, work ethic, or native intelligence, but you can develop skills. For example, the US Navy spends years training fighter pilots. But how about the personnel on aircraft carrier decks who launch the screaming jets into the air with steam catapults? Some load high explosives while others taxi the aircraft. These extremely hazardous positions require expert abilities, but the Navy qualifies sailors to perform these jobs in less than a year. These twenty-somethings play supersonic dodgeball with 30-ton war machines on a frenzied air station smaller than a football field. Remember this next time you're tempted to run a recruiting ad that requires five years of experience and a master's degree.

Too many business owners overestimate the benefits of previous work experience and underestimate the power of character, training, and culture. Experience can create value, but only some kinds of experience in some situations. Just because people have been doing a job for a long time does not mean they have been doing it well. Surprisingly often, I have found that experienced people from other companies were unable to perform our jobs well after we hired them. For many roles, it's much more important to hire a person of great potential than a person with great experience.

You can teach people to drive but you can't teach them to have drive. You can coach skills but not character. Someone who has demonstrated good judgment and the ability to work well with others will most likely continue to demonstrate those qualities. This same principle applies to negative traits.

Match the personality to the role. You won't alter a person's fundamental characteristics. Look for a naturally bubbly personality for a greeter, or a meticulous person for accounting. Psychologists have identified various forms of intelligence, including verbal, emotional, kinesthetic, mathematical, and more. There are many ways to be smart, so look for the kind of mental faculties a position requires. For example, successful auto technicians don't require advanced interpersonal communication skills, but they do require excellent hand-eye coordination and spatial thinking ability.

Identify and never ignore red flags. Rely on your intuition and processes to identify the people who are impolite, disrespectful, unprepared, incompetent, or difficult, and don't hire them—no matter what! When evaluating a candidate, ask yourself:

- *Would I enjoy working with her?*
- *Would she feel bad if she let someone down?*
- *Will she follow through on her commitments?*
- *Does she share our values?*
- *Does she have the mental firepower to do the job?*

Hang on to the good people you already have. Retaining your solid performers beats trying to hire new ones. Ensure that their pay is competitive. Tell them how much you appreciate their contributions. If they are special, do special things for them.

A poor hiring process leads to poor hiring. Before we developed a robust process, we hired some people who couldn't show why they deserved to be on our team, or even show up for work at all. Right after we opened, desperate for salespeople, I remember interviewing an applicant and offering him a job right on the spot after I concluded his first and only interview. We set up a start date based on a two-week notice that he would give his employer. We shook hands and I looked forward to him joining the team. The start date came, but he didn't show up. I called him to see if there was some confusion, but he never called me back. My feelings were hurt and I was angry with him, but I realized my flimsy hiring system was the problem. Many applicants don't have the character and professionalism to work at Planet, and it's my job to find those who do. When I look back on my professional mistakes, this might be my favorite failure because it taught me that we couldn't rely on just my instincts to properly evaluate applicants—we needed a real system.

A Simple, Effective Hiring Process

In your recruiting ads, ask all applicants to submit a resume and cover letter. In our experience, a surprisingly large number of people omit the cover letter, which tells us something about their ability to follow instructions. Of those who include a cover letter, most are generic, and that's okay. Rarely, a few people wow us with language that describes how our unusual business model appeals to them. We hire a surprisingly high percentage of these applicants, not because we care that much about cover letters, but because we discovered that the person who invests the time to learn about our company and express a passion for our values will likely succeed with us. Cover letters often reveal more about an applicant than the resume.

Create a list of answers to frequently asked questions. Early on, our ads invited applicants to call me with any questions. I was spending hours a day answering repetitive queries such as, "What's a typical day on the job like?" Eventually, I realized I could automate this by sending FAQs in a response email to qualified candidates. In this email, we invite candidates to call after they review the information to learn more about the position and our company. Most never call, and that's good, because we let the majority of candidates filter themselves out, rather than tax our resources to evaluate every person who applies.

When candidates call, conduct a brief, informal phone screening. Do they meet a minimum threshold of professionalism? For example, can they communicate clearly on the phone? Have they taken the time to learn more about our company by visiting our website? Are they enthusiastic about our business philosophy? We don't want to set the bar too high here, but we don't want it too low, either, because we only have so much time for interviews and we want to focus on candidates who show the most promise.

Conduct three interviews before hiring candidates. Multiple interviews provide more opportunities for unprofessional people to reveal their bad habits. If applicants can't show up punctually three times in a row, for example, how likely are they to arrive promptly after they join the team? Also, repeated introductions and exposure to the business on different occasions give candidates a more accurate impression of what the job is and isn't, so they can decide whether the position is right for them. In our first interview, one manager assesses if there's enough potential to justify consuming the time of additional team members. The second interview replaces the first manager with two or three others. We call the third interview a shadow day, where candidates spend the day observing how we do business. They can acquire a clear understanding of what they will be doing once they join us. They meet our front-line team members. We later invite all the people in that department to offer their input before we hire.

Always involve several team members in the interviewing process. Your team will appreciate that you considered their opinions, and sometimes they will catch red flags you missed, saving you from expensive hiring mistakes.

Use the same set of questions for all candidates applying for the same position. Unless you use organized scripts, you can fall into the trap of spending your precious time talking about things that have little to do with the job, such as hobbies. We identified the key characteristics we need to see in Planet team members, and we ask the candidates questions about how they have demonstrated those qualities in previous jobs or school. These structured interviews produce answers with high "signal value" about who the candidates really are. We don't use any goofy puzzles or trick questions—just straightforward inquiries about the person's instincts and habits.

Invite candidates to interview you while you interview them. Encourage them to ask lots of questions. We want to reduce the number of hires who quickly quit because they didn't understand the responsibilities, pace, culture, or challenges. They need to see the full picture, warts and all. We can learn only so much about a candidate during three interviews, so we need their help in determining whether or not there's a good fit.

Ask candidates to follow up with you. Throughout the process, ask them to call you to set up the next step rather than volunteering to call them. We end each interview with the same request: "After you've had an opportunity overnight to consider what we've discussed today, please call tomorrow to set up the next interview." This creates additional opportunities to observe how well they follow instructions, and you'll save time by not pursuing candidates who have lost interest. We want to see that candidates have the professionalism to pick up the phone and get things done. If they can't do that during the hiring process, when they know their behavior is under scrutiny, they probably won't do it after we hire them.

Pick soldiers, not people who look good in a uniform. Focus primarily on skills that the job requires, not interview skills or a good resume. Don't fall for the applicants who dress the best, went to a fancy school, or just happen to hit it off with you. Don't put too much stock in these things unless the job demands them. Ultimately, you need someone to excel on the job, not dazzle you during an interview. We have hired several people who performed terribly during their interviews, and they are still with us doing good work. We know what we're looking for, and don't really care if they know all the rules about interviewing. Many applicants for blue-collar positions, for example, never had the opportunity to develop interview skills, so we're more interested in assessing the actual strengths needed for the position. Introverts, who might bring desirable traits to your team, typically do not shine in traditional interview situations. I recommend Susan Cain's book, *Quiet*, to anyone conducting interviews so they can better appreciate this half of the population and put their useful skills to work on your team.

Move quickly and don't jerk candidates around. If you take too long to make a decision, some candidates will accept another offer rather than wait for one you may never make. I remember once postponing an interview for a week because I was headed out of town. In the meantime, the candidate accepted a sales position at another dealership. Fortunately, we both left the door open, and he realized his mistake once he had spent a week in a typical dealership. He would become our number one volume salesperson before we promoted him. We almost missed him entirely. Remember what it was like when you were looking for a job. Be responsive and kind, for your benefit and theirs.

After hiring, provide them with the training they need to succeed. Because we attract most of our workforce from outside the industry, we need to train new hires extensively. In most dealerships, new salespeople get a stack of brochures, instructions to follow around an experienced salesperson for a day, and that's about it. No wonder the annual turnover in automotive retail exceeds 67 percent. We spend weeks training our new hires before they talk to the first customer, helping them with product knowledge and role-playing the situations they'll encounter often. We developed this regimen organically through the years, and we created our own internal training manual because there was nothing off the shelf that fit our unique sales process. We rotate the new hires through days with the sales managers, which is disruptive and challenging to organize in a busy retail environment, but far superior to cutting people loose without the skills and confidence to succeed.

Expanding Your Talent Pool

Nationwide, less than 20 percent of the people who work at dealerships are women, but at Planet Subaru, they make up a third of our team, with at least one woman in every department. They include five managers, nine women in sales, and many in the service department, including the service manager and the majority of our advisors. We have six women turning wrenches as technicians—more than any other dealership of any brand or size in the United States.

People ask how we got to a total of thirty women on our team in a male-dominated industry. Well, we had twenty-nine, and then we hired one more! Seriously, we've been using that one-at-a-time strategy since we hired our first saleswoman upon opening in 1998. At some point, we achieved a critical mass, so a woman rarely finds herself the only one in the room. It's not uncommon to see the service manager and shop manager huddling with a couple technicians over an engine— and they're all women.

One of our technicians wrote this to us: "During my first interview, I shared my goal of being a master tech. I expected to hear all about how difficult and time-consuming that would be. But you told me that you would help me do it. Part of why I love working here so much is because you took a chance on me when no one else would. I wanted so badly to just get my foot in the door in the automotive field, but I couldn't do that without prior experience at a dealership. You welcomed me with open arms and I am so grateful for this opportunity. I work hard to be a role model for my son and try my best to prove that I deserve to be here and I am a good technician, not just good 'for a girl.'"

Here are some excuses I've heard for not hiring more women, and why I think they miss the mark:

"Women don't apply for our openings." We don't see enough applicants either, but we include language like this in our recruiting ads: "Women and other people from backgrounds traditionally excluded from retail automotive careers constitute the majority of our team. We encourage you to apply. We will train." Some of our team members tell us they applied because they were specifically invited, and they wanted to work where others like them were already succeeding.

"Even when we find a good female candidate, she won't take the job." Beyond income and traditional benefits, do you offer enough reasons to join your team? Are your schedules flexible? Do your pay plans provide a secure level of income? Does your workplace culture welcome women? You may want to adopt more progressive personnel policies to turn appli-can'ts into appli-cans.

"We can't find experienced or qualified women." There aren't many women in our industry, so we look for women with experience in a related field and then train them our way. One of our technicians was building furniture. Our shop manager was running a gym. You might struggle to find, say, an experienced female service manager—unless you can continually develop and promote your own superstar cashier, which is how we did it.

"They might get pregnant and leave." They might, but we've yet to lose a team member to pregnancy—all have returned after leave. And even if one did, men leave for a thousand reasons too. We have ten moms on our team, and moms make things happen. On the afternoon our service manager delivered her second child, she was working at the counter with customers, gritting through contractions while she waited for her husband to arrive and take her to the hospital!

Conscious Unhiring

Not every hire will succeed, so firing people is sometimes necessary, as painful as it is for everyone involved. It's no fun to take away a person's income and job identity, even if only temporarily. Fortunately, we don't need to fire people very often for the following reasons:

The fewer the mistakes made hiring, the fewer the people who need firing.

Performance-based pay plans encourage underperforming people to figure out for themselves that they're not in the right situation, because they don't earn enough to want to stay on our team. They often decide to quit on their own.

Before we even think about termination, we are quite patient with team members who are struggling to master skills. Especially when they join us from outside the industry, some take a year or more to get the hang of a position. We invest significantly in hiring and training, so we don't want to let someone go before exhausting every effort to improve their abilities. We try to retrain them, focusing on the areas where they're underperforming.

Sometimes someone really needs to go, however, and I'm hardly the only business owner guilty of keeping underperformers around too long. It's hard to fire a friend. I remember a fellow dealer who was unsatisfied with his service manager. Over a couple of years, I asked him a few times how he was handling the situation. The manager was unintentionally sabotaging the whole business, including chasing off good technicians and alienating customers. It was obvious to me—and everybody else—that the owner needed to fire him, but the two were close personally. After he finally acted, I asked my friend how he felt. "There was no way to avoid firing him, so I should have done it a long time ago." If it's not going to work out, the sooner you end it, the better. I muster the strength to do the hard, right thing by looking at how a poor performer impacts all the other people who depend on our business for their livelihoods. It's not fair for one person to interfere with the whole team's ability to provide for their families. And sometimes, firing people helps them find jobs better suited to their personalities, with tasks they enjoy more.

When it becomes clear that a person isn't measuring up, we usually set a concrete, reasonable bar of performance required by a certain time, usually ninety days. Occasionally people rise to the challenge, as the glimpse of losing a place on the team motivates them to find another gear. But other times we need to have the difficult conversation. We open it with, "Do you know why we're talking today?" The person usually responds with something like, "You gave me a standard to meet, I didn't meet it, so I guess that means I can't work here anymore." At that point you're just agreeing with them instead of digging into difficult topics. The expectations were set clearly ahead of time, and they know they didn't meet them.

We always have a minimum of two managers present in case there's ever a question about what was said, and we try not to get involved in any lengthy conversations that rehash the past, since the decision to separate has already been made.

We aim to conduct these conversations in a way that eases the pain and allows them to walk out with their heads held high. We don't even use the word "fire." Instead, we say, "We've decided that today is going to be your last day here." We want to treat them humanely and preserve whatever remains of the relationship. We would prefer that they don't sue or cause other kinds of problems, and they would generally prefer to avoid a confrontation that burns a bridge.

Compensation

I knew a parts director who was getting paid approximately $175,000 a year at another dealership, probably close to double the competitive rate for a department of that size. This occurred because the dealership owner neglected to update the manager's pay plan on an annual basis, and as the dealership grew due to rapid population growth in the area, so did the director's pay. Eventually, business slowed down, forcing the dealership owner to reduce expenses to keep the dealership profitable. He told the director that his new pay plan would deliver about $100,000 per year, still a generous income by competitive standards, but substantially less than he had earned in recent years. He quit on the spot, after more than twenty years there, confident he could make $175,000 or more elsewhere. As his income had increased, so did the cost of his lifestyle. He couldn't afford to live on $100,000 anymore. But once he started looking for another job, the director discovered that no one wanted to hire him at $175,000, or even $100,000. Desperate after several months of unemployment, he took a lesser position for $80,000. A few years later, he returned to the original dealership as a parts director earning $100,000, the same amount that caused him to quit in the first place.

People are not the rational decision makers imagined by some economists. Sometimes pay discussions involve psychological entanglements beyond the reach of reason.

Various dynamics can complicate a worker's relationship with pay, such as their family relationships. Money troubles at home can become your problem to address if the team member's household spends more than you're paying. Even after a quarter century in business, I still haven't figured it out perfectly. But I have learned this much:

Deal with any compensation matters immediately and seriously. If you make a commitment, follow through on it to the letter. If your accounting office makes a mistake, correct it as soon as you learn about it. Few things will upset a team member more than feeling slighted in their compensation, so don't let any issues fester.

Avoid surprises and give people some warning if their pay needs to change. We write into every pay plan that we will review it at least annually. If we see a change is needed the following year, we prefer to alert the team member in the autumn that a change is coming in January. We try to communicate why we need to pay a competitive wage for that position—even during boom times—so the business is positioned to survive the tough times.

Exercise caution with bonuses. My friend owns a business and gives a costly annual holiday bonus to everyone based on the profitability of the dealership that year. Unfortunately, some of his people have come to take it for granted, limiting any motivational effect. Worse, after a tough year, those people see the decline in bonus from the previous year as a pay cut and grumble about it.

Don't underpay people. Some of your people will never ask for a raise, even though they deserve one. Paying them competitively reduces the likelihood that they give their notice out of the blue after finding a bigger paycheck elsewhere. You build trust with team members when you increase pay (even modestly) without making them ask.

Don't overpay people. To survive and thrive, businesses need to maintain healthy levels of personnel expense. People work for a variety of reasons, and the amount of compensation is more relevant to some people than others. You don't necessarily need to pay more than another company to attract and retain good people. As long as your compensation is competitive, people will consider other factors when deciding to join or stay with your team. However, as we have grown, we have decided to share some of our additional revenue with our team. We can afford to pay our people a little more than our competitors, so we do. This is one more reason that we have almost no turnover.

Pay attention to what you pay. At least annually, look at a report of compensation amounts for everyone on your team to make sure you're not underpaying or overpaying anyone. Perhaps you'll find someone whose job responsibilities or hours increased or decreased, creating a gap between their earnings and their contributions. Or you might discover gender or minority disparities that need to be corrected. I would guess that very few businesses intentionally create those situations, but they can develop for more benign reasons. For example, in the absence of a formal pay scale that big corporations might use, a smaller company might bring a woman on board at a salary higher than her last position, but still below a man's in a similar job role.

Designing Pay Plans

We pay most of our people using performance-based pay plans, as opposed to straight salary. Here's why:

While salary plans are simpler to create, administer, and understand, they do not reward the worker for doing exceptional work. They financially isolate workers from the problems they might be causing, forcing managers to intervene externally. Beneficially, however, they do protect team members from swings caused by variables outside their control.

Performance pay plans reward a team member's output, motivating behavior with financial rewards. They expose people to the discomfort of a smaller paycheck when productivity declines. Also, performance pay plans tend to float your personnel expense with the tide of business conditions; they pay more during good times when you can afford it, and less during business downturns when you can't.

Disadvantages of performance pay plans include vulnerability to uncomfortable swings from year to year, and the difficulty of minimizing impacts caused by outside factors, such as a boom or a recession.

Design your pay plans the way you might stick your head into the mouth of an alligator: very carefully. Ignore psychological factors at your peril. Look at the chart below and note that with the more volatile Pay Plan #2, the team member made more money over time.

Pay Plan #1	Year	Pay Plan #2
$80,000	2018	$75,000
$83,000	2019	$120,000
$86,000	2020	$80,000
$89,000	2021	$85,000
$338,000	Total	$360,000

Given the choice, you would expect most people to be happier with the second pay plan, because it ends up paying substantially more ($22,000) than the first. But the large fluctuations will, for most people, cause more problems than the extra money solves. Even if lucky external business conditions caused the big upswing in 2019, people will naturally feel they "earned" every penny of the increase because they showed up every day and worked hard the whole year. People will experience a sense of loss when their pay declines going into the next year, and they usually don't understand that businesses with slim margins can't remain viable by giving permanent raises like that. And since a surprising number of people live paycheck to paycheck (even high earners), the joys associated with a fat 2019 don't compensate for a slimmer check arriving every week of 2020. A spouse at home struggling with these adjustments can compound the anxiety.

You avoid some of these problems with pay plans that take the following factors into account:

The performance of the individual team member should influence rewards more than external factors, such as how well the business is doing overall.

Ideally, team members should experience smooth, steady growth in their income over time. Try to avoid creating a plan with large swings from year to year.

Pay any bonuses relatively often so your people experience the enjoyment more frequently, reinforcing the desired behavior. Monthly bonuses are better than annual bonuses.

Align your pay with the mission you want your people to execute. For example, we want our salespeople focused on sales volume and customer satisfaction, so we pay on both. Were we to pay just on sales, we would reward them to take on additional customers instead of focusing on the needs of the customers they already have.

If circumstances cause a pay plan to fall outside a sensible range (high or low), then act quickly to revise it, knowing that any discomfort associated with the difficult conversation will only grow with procrastination.

Profit Wise Questions

- Do you have a hiring system? Is it documented in any way? Does everyone involved in hiring understand what it is?

- If you could wave a magic wand and attract any kind of team members you want, who would they be? Do you use any methods to identify these people?

- Are there patterns in your hiring successes and failures? (For example, do you consistently lose people in the first ninety days?) How might you change your process to better reveal the personal qualities that drive those successful or unsuccessful patterns before you hire?

- Do your recruiting ads stand out in any positive way from your competition's? Are you warmly inviting candidates who are traditionally overlooked to apply?

- Do your pay plans reward your best performers for accomplishing the goals you determined? Do you know if you're paying anyone too little or too much?

Online Resources

This book comes with a detailed worksheet to help you develop effective pay plans, samples of our recruiting ads, an example of an outstanding applicant cover letter, and interview script templates. Find them at jeffmorrill.com/reader-tools.

CHAPTER 4

Leading the Team

What is leadership? At a fundamental level, it's the ability to organize others in pursuit of a common purpose. However, that hardly tells the whole story, because leadership isn't a single skill, but a comprehensive capacity. Leadership aptitude is a cluster of talents, qualities, and experience, so instead of trying to characterize leadership with statements or sentences, we prefer to identify it by asking questions that detect its presence. When it's time to decide whether to promote our team members into supervisory roles, we need to make accurate predictions about how well they can lead other people to success.

We ask ourselves the following questions about team members in two broad categories of character and skills:

Character:

- Do they believe and live our core values?
- Do they do what they say they will do? Do they walk their own talk?
- Do they inspire trust in others? Can other people count on them?
- Do they earn the respect of those who interact with them?
- Do they consistently manage their emotions well?
- Do they instinctively care for the needs of others when making decisions?
- Do they have the will to do the right thing even if it's unpopular?

Skills:

- Can they identify problems and envision solutions?
- Do they have the formal and informal communication skills to share that vision?
- Can they plan the work and then work the plan?
- Can they delegate effectively, and inspect what they expect?
- Can they make prompt, thoughtful decisions and accept good advice?
- Are they organized enough to follow through on their commitments?
- Can they help others improve through inspiration rather than fear?
- Can they resolve disputes among team members?
- Are they comfortable carrying the responsibility of command?

Occasionally we face a dilemma when a position opens before a person has developed all these qualities. In those cases, we need to answer the question of whether leadership qualities are innate, or if they can be acquired through training and experience. We believe we can mentor people who have enough motivation and the right kinds of intelligence. For example, if their prior educational or work experience did not endow them with excellent communication skills, we've had success coaching them up to an acceptable level.

However, any significant concerns about character will disqualify a team member from consideration, because we recognize how unlikely it is to change a person's fundamental qualities. For example, we learned the hard way that members who lose control of their emotions and treat others without respect cannot be eligible for promotion, no matter how talented they might be.

In the rest of this chapter, I'll share the skills that we nurture in our leaders. They fall into three categories: building trust, motivating the team, and maintaining a healthy culture.

Building Trust

Set a good example. Your team has many eyes, and they watch you closely. If, as Ralph Waldo Emerson wrote, an institution is the "lengthened shadow of one person," it's because people naturally take cues from their leader. Your people will figure out sooner or later whether you're living your life in harmony with the values you espouse. That means you have to follow your own rules and keep your promises, even the little ones about seemingly insignificant things (like calling back today or sending an email this week).

Earn respect based on your actions and reactions. The essence of trust is the feeling that people and circumstances are predictable in a positive way—and that goes for a leader's mood, too. Emotional energy is extremely contagious, and you have a responsibility to manage yours to protect others. Dwight Eisenhower said, "You don't lead by hitting people over the head—that's assault, not leadership." Your role requires you to keep your wits when others lose theirs. Because fear exerts an immediate impact on human behavior, weak leaders manage by bullying. They intimidate team members and threaten their employment. Few people will consistently deliver good results under these conditions. Your best performers will leave in search of more sophisticated leadership, and you'll smother the morale of those who remain.

Keep your ego in check. You may play a big role in the success of your company, but beware of getting caught up in your own public relations or inhaling your own fumes. At the end of the chess match, the kings and the pawns all go in the same box. You're a critical team member, but still just part of the team. You might run with the movers and shakers, but there will always be someone smarter, richer, or more accomplished than you. Don't organize your sense of self around the size of your boat or the amount of money you throw around. If you must seek approval, you'll command greater admiration by conducting yourself as a decent person with a modest sense of your accomplishments.

Stop talking. Most businesspeople don't shut up long enough to put their listening skills to work. It's easy to become infatuated with your ideas, stories, and the sound of your own voice. If you surround yourself with people who obtain some kind of financial benefit from their relationship with you, they will generally laugh at your dumb jokes and give you the encouragement to keep talking—but you're not learning anything when your mouth is moving. Leave some conversational oxygen for others. Remember the acronym WAIT: Why Am I Talking? When you catch yourself talking too much or not listening enough, invite other opinions and ask thoughtful questions to draw others out. Set aside your phone and other distractions when your team members are talking to you. Just because your body is present doesn't mean your full attention is, and people know the difference.

Don't lie to anybody, about big things or little things. When people hear you lying to others, they come to suspect that you might someday lie to them. You don't need to show all your cards to everybody all the time, but you shouldn't make a habit of intentionally deceiving people. Most people lie out of laziness. With some effort, you can almost always find a way to communicate just as effectively in an honest manner. Lie only under exceptional circumstances, when you have exhausted all other alternatives.

Roll up your sleeves once in a while to show solidarity with your team. Remind yourself how challenging it is to do the work your team does every day. During big snowstorms that dumped several feet of snow on our ten acres and five hundred cars, I would make it a point to show up in snow gear and work among our team to help clear the lot. When people see that you care enough to do hard work, they'll care more too. And you might come away with ideas to improve your operations.

Be kind to everybody. As a respected leader in your organization, your simple gestures will have a big effect on your team. Even when doing tough things, like firing people, you can speak gently and let them leave with dignity. During those difficult conversations, even when I thought the people had really wronged me or the team, I made a point of thanking them for the positive things they did for us during their tenure.

Assume positive intent on the part of your team members. Because of the cognitive bias known as "fundamental attribution error," we tend to assume that someone's behavior entirely reflects their intentions, and we don't adequately consider all the external circumstances. Some managers see people making mistakes and assume they are idiots or that they don't care. A variety of other reasons can explain mistakes, including insufficient training or flawed systems. As author Jane West wrote, "Let us not attribute to malice and cruelty what may be referred to less criminal motives." At Planet, we assume you care passionately about doing a good job, so when a mistake occurs, we rarely approach it as a disciplinary event.

Hold people accountable instead of punishing them. We help our people understand the connection between a mistake and its consequences. We do this confidentially, obeying the parenting maxim about praising in public and correcting in private. Once, a technician left a sharp tool in the back seat of a customer's car. The customer found it before his toddler did, avoiding any injury. We shared this information with the technician, who felt bad enough to redouble his future efforts to clear cars of tools after completing the work. No punishment was needed, and we obtained a much better outcome without it. Occasionally someone might make a serious error in judgment that requires a forceful response, such as a written warning not to repeat an egregious failure—but you can handle even these incidents in a corrective rather than punitive fashion. Holding people accountable for their actions doesn't require punishment, and punishment doesn't always hold people accountable. Beating on somebody might temporarily relieve your frustration, but that won't necessarily modify future behavior if you don't address the underlying causes.

Invest in remedies rather than assigning blame. During my early days working at Don Beyer, I was helping move cars at their new Land Rover dealership. Unfamiliar with the unusual transmission in a Defender, I rolled one down a hill into a brand-new Range Rover. When I delivered the bad news to the manager, I was expecting an earful. He almost cried when he saw the pile of twisted British iron, but he didn't yell at me. He immediately figured out that whoever had last parked the Defender did not leave the differentials engaged properly. He went back in and asked each individual on the team to avoid parking a Defender in that mode again. Nowadays, when our team members damage vehicles on the lot, we ask them to report it immediately and we give them immunity from any punishment. People make mistakes, and as long as they don't keep making them, it's best to give them a little grace.

Empower your front-line people to solve problems and make their own decisions. Some CEOs collect millions of dollars in annual compensation and fly around on private jets, but don't give their customer-facing workers the ability to spend a hundred bucks to solve a simple problem or make a customer happy. Among other liberties, our front-line team members can refund the cost of a service, buy lunch for a waiting customer, or include a detailed cleaning of a car without seeking permission.

Communicate relentlessly. Your people need to know what you want them to do and why they need to do it. As an executive, you might thrive under conditions of uncertainty, but most people don't like surprises. When you need to make changes, make sure the affected people know as soon as possible. When you have time to prepare, include some or all of the team members in formulating the plan. You can do this formally, via meetings or email, or informally, by soliciting input in the lunch room or on the shop floor.

Motivating Your Team

You can pay people to show up, but you have to earn their hearts. Before I had much experience supervising other people, I naively thought that sufficient training, encouragement, and financial compensation would automatically motivate them to maintain a high level of performance. But to obtain the best from your team, you need to consistently find ways to renew their enthusiasm for the job and keep them focused on their tasks and results. People respond differently to a wide variety of incentives. Consider all these things that propel some people, but not others: bonuses, verbal praise, status, recognition, titles, awards, time off, gifts, perks, food, promotions, and more. Each individual requires a unique approach.

Celebrate victories. People need frequent encouragement and reinforcement to perform at their best, so we recognize the wins without making too much of a fuss. One of our favorites is a lunch-time pizza party to celebrate a promotion or a dealership award. Also, doing occasional, non-mandatory fun things outside work helps people get to know each other better. For example, we occasionally host department dinners out at a restaurant so team members can meet each other's spouses or partners.

Affirm and recognize. Team members really appreciate genuine praise or a handwritten thank you note from the boss. With compliments, the more you give away, the richer you get. A little love and attention from the leader go a long way. I enjoy catching our people doing things right, so when I phone in and get that friendly "Welcome to Planet," I acknowledge the team member's enthusiasm. When I overhear a manager working with an upset customer and turning a frown upside down, I compliment her afterwards. When industry associations offer awards, I nominate our most qualified people. They often win, but even when they don't, they still appreciate the kind words. People take the occasional pill of constructive criticism more readily when they eat a steady diet of affirmation and recognition.

Resist the temptation to micromanage, interfere, and second-guess. General George S. Patton said, "Never tell people how to do things. Tell them what to do and they will surprise you with their ingenuity." You dramatically increase the likelihood of success when the people closest to the problem participate fully in a plan. There are often multiple solutions to a problem, none dramatically better than another, so even if your team wants to zig while you want to zag, they might get to the same destination anyway. Founders naturally struggle with the transition from the start-up days—when they had their hands on every activity—to a mature company where managers do the work. You can coach your team, but let them solve problems on their own. If you still have to make all the decisions, you're holding them and your company back.

Be there for your people when it matters most. When our mother died in 1996, my brother was working at the Ford

Motor Company Mid-Atlantic Headquarters in Virginia. His regional manager drove four hours to attend the funeral in Blacksburg, expressed his condolences, and then turned around and drove the four hours back. He gave up a day of his life to pay his respects. My brother was touched, and so was I. He and John remain friends to this day. That manager would go on to lead Hyundai Motor America as CEO, and decades later, whenever I run into him at professional events, I thank him for his support of our family during that time. I don't like funerals, but whenever a team member loses a close family member, I make it a priority to go, and I write a letter to the family. When our team members need special help, perhaps after running out of paid leave for an illness, we find a way to get them through. Sometimes people need a "hand up" when they're facing health problems, divorces, sick kids, financial difficulties, and other challenges. If you've selected them well, your people won't forget the help they got when they needed it.

Make changes at a sustainable pace. Don't burn your people out with more change than they can handle at a time. Even positive changes in procedures, facilities, or personnel upset the status quo and cause some level of anxiety. Thanks to exceptional leadership under CEO Tom Doll, Subaru has been growing consistently, with national sales tripling over a decade. Managing all that growth has required us to double the size of our team and undertake major facility upgrades (while continuing to operate during the construction). To prevent everyone from losing their minds, we try to limit the amount of simultaneous changes we make. For example, our hiring process demands the efforts of multiple team members, so we try to focus on one opening at a time, choosing the position in greatest need and moving on to the next after we make a hire.

Maintaining a Healthy Culture

What is culture? It's what your people do when you're not looking. This is why management guru Peter Drucker said that "culture eats strategy for breakfast." You can't teach someone what to do in every situation, so your people will act on their values and training when making decisions.

Show your appreciation when team members have a new idea or disagree with you. What behaviors are rewarded in your organization? Most corporations lose their agility as they grow because their cultures come to privilege conformity over healthy risk-taking. My brother worked in a staid corporate culture at Ford Motor Company for over a decade and saw how established companies come to discourage alternative viewpoints. Seek dissenting opinions and encourage independent thinkers.

Mentor your people and urge them to do the same. Just as parents pass values along to their children, mentors pass along the company's values to rising stars. Mentoring is a powerful diffuser of knowledge and talent, so reward people for taking colleagues under their wings. At Planet, each department manager has a second-in-command who performs the manager's role in his or her absence. This pairing creates a natural advisor relationship that allows both people to grow their skills together.

Spend some time every week on foot patrol. Leave the ivory tower of your office long enough to walk around and observe how your business actually runs. Put your experienced eyes on things and talk with your team and customers. People will appreciate the genuine interest you show in them.

Use words intentionally. Words matter because language shapes the way we think. Our salespeople are Purchase Partners because they help you buy a car, not try to stick you into one. We don't have employees—we have team members, because we gather together in common purpose to accomplish goals. The numerous female members of our team are women, not girls. Other retail automotive outlets are dealerships; we are the alternative to all the typical showroom shenanigans. We're your *un*dealership.

Be cautious with outside executives. Former House Speaker Sam Rayburn said, "A jackass can kick down a barn but it takes a carpenter to build one." It's the same for your culture—the wrong hire can cause significant damage. The more authority given to a position, the more harm outside hires can do to your culture, because they have more power to screw things up. We believe in growing and promoting our own team members so we know exactly what kind of people are making the important decisions for the company. Plus, morale increases when your people see a meritocratic path to advancement. Since new hires are unknown quantities, we prefer to bring them in at entry-level positions, where we can immerse them in our ways of doing things, and then let the cream rise to the top. As these team members earn management positions, we know they'll see and do things the Planet way.

The work of building your culture is never done. Just as an abandoned field will eventually turn to weeds without a farmer's care, your culture requires a constant input of energy and wise decisions to remain productive. Here is an example:

Most of the used vehicles that customers trade in for new ones have hit everything but the lottery, so we don't offer them for retail sale. We "wholesale" them out to small used car dealers. Mike (I changed his name for privacy) used to buy the majority of these cars.

From our first meeting, he rubbed me the wrong way. He was a little too confident and complimentary. He talked about unprofessional things. To disguise the smell of cigarette smoke, he doused himself with Fahrenheit cologne. When he sat in a chair, the wallet in his back pocket caused him to list like an old ship. It was fat with business cards, receipts—everything but money.

There's a term of art in the car business that describes well-worn vehicles with odometer failures: true mileage unknown. We also use it as euphemism to describe a person rough around the edges, and Mike was definitely TMU. The car business has cleaned itself up somewhat over the last few decades, but substance abuse and dishonesty can still make the low end of the used car business a little shady. Mike didn't really stand out relative to other personalities we encounter in the wholesale world, but I wouldn't have wanted to interact with him every day. However, our managing partner, Dale Lathrop, got along with him okay. They were friendly enough that Dale even invited him to an Independence Day party at his house. Mike showed up with enough fireworks to fill the entire cargo area of an SUV and put on a forty-five-minute show.

At some point, Mike asked for one of our black team jackets that featured all of our Planet embroidery. We don't sell our logo clothing. The only way to get a Planet jacket is to clear the high hurdle of joining our team, or to receive one as a VIP gift. I wasn't crazy about the idea of Mike visiting other dealerships with our jacket, concerned that people might think he worked for us. After all, I invested years of my life in building the reputation behind those Planet trademarks. I didn't trust Mike, I didn't like him, and I didn't want to be around him. But he paid us a little more for cars than other wholesalers, and since we liquidate hundreds of those cars each year, that money can really add up. Perhaps I was blinded by the dollar signs in my eyes, like you see in old cartoons when the character gets too excited about money. I agreed to give him a jacket.

During that time, in 2012 and 2013, buildings were burning down left and right in our community, Boston's South Shore. Marinas, warehouses, offices, apartments—someone set fire to thirty buildings over the span of a couple years. It seemed like you couldn't pick up a paper or turn on the news without learning about another inferno. It was a miracle no one got killed or injured. The fires were frequent and random enough that I had some concerns about our building.

One day, two state police officers showed up with a warrant to look at all of our vehicle sales records. They told us that some of the vehicles that customers had traded in to us—and which we had wholesaled out—were spotted near the scenes of some of these crimes. They told us that they suspected Mike, and they warned him that they were watching him. They installed GPS tracking devices on the vehicles he was driving so they could monitor his whereabouts. Buildings kept burning, and the police finally gathered enough evidence to arrest him. He had been committing all these crimes driving the vehicles we had sold him, wearing our Planet Subaru jacket! As if that weren't bad enough, after his arrest we would learn that he had defrauded us of over $20,000 by stealing vehicle titles.

Though Mike probably set all the fires, the state only had enough evidence to convict on a few. The judge sentenced him to an outrageously brief two years in prison, during which time the fire chiefs across the South Shore breathed a sigh of relief. Almost immediately upon his release, four more buildings burned, and the police arrested him again. The prosecutor described Mike's confession: "Some people, when they're stressed, they drink; some people, when they're stressed, get into fights. Mike said that when he gets stressed, he starts fires."

While the courts were just as slow as Dale and I to reckon with Mike's dangerous behavior, they eventually caught on, too. The judge sentenced him to another ten to fifteen years.

Dale and I paid a high price to learn several lessons, but learn them we did:

- Follow your intuition when establishing business relationships with people outside your company. Vet them just as thoroughly as job applicants, because key people, both on and off your payroll, can cause a lot of problems.

- Culture is not a "plant-it-and-forget-it" proposition. A forest that took decades to grow can be burned down surprisingly quickly if you bring in the wrong people or lose sight of what makes your company special in the first place.

- And if a guy shows up to your house party with 400 Roman candles, he just might be a pyromaniac.

After we cleaned up that mess, we revamped our wholesale liquidation process to put Planet people in charge. One of our sales managers, a Villanova mathematics graduate, now uses online software to cut out the shady middlemen; he auctions the cars directly to dealerships in any state. We make more money on each wholesale car, which allows us to give customers more money for their trade-ins, so we're selling more cars than ever. The whole time that we were exposing the company to significant risk in pursuit of a little extra money, there was a more profitable solution in total harmony with our values, right under our nose. I'll never again put short-term profits ahead of the long-term interests of the company.

Profit Wise Questions

- What is your definition of leadership?
- Do you and your managers walk your own talk?
- If everybody in your company acted the way you do, what kind of company would you have?
- Would you want to work for someone like you? What qualities make you difficult? What can you

do to isolate your people from those issues or negative emotions?

- Do you have any jerks in leadership positions? (Hopefully you're not one of them!) What are you doing about that?

- Do you talk too much or not listen enough?

- Are you and your managers mentoring the next generation of leaders in your company?

CHAPTER 5

Marketing

Copywriter Walter Bernbach said, "If your advertising goes unnoticed, everything else is academic." In other words, your business will suffer if you can't figure out a way to communicate effectively with likely purchasers.

Businesses in the US spend billions of dollars each year trying to get people to buy things. You encounter hundreds, perhaps thousands of marketing messages every day: social media ads, radio ads in the car, brand badges on vehicles, banner ads on websites, logos on clothing, wraps on buses, screens at the gas pump, and more. In a world short on attention and long on advertising, how do you make your message stand out?

Start With a Good Business Name

Your business name communicates ideas, feelings, and related thoughts to prospective customers whenever they hear it or read it. Is your company sober and secure, hip and edgy, elite and upscale, or approachable and friendly? Your company name appears everywhere in your marketing and delivers the first impression of your business. It might be one of the most significant marketing decisions you ever make. (If you're already operating a business, it probably won't make sense to change your name, so you might want to add or revise your slogan instead.)

Consider these four key factors before choosing your name:

Is it memorable? We chose Planet because we liked the connotations of earth-friendliness, large size, and contemporary vibe. And it definitely stood out from other dealerships named after the town or owner.

Is it web-friendly? Ideally your URL is available without resorting to confusing variations, such as planet-subaru-auto-dealership.net. In a crowded field of competitors, a geographic name like Boston Widget Repair could put your company at the top of a search results page when someone searches "widget repair in Boston."

Is it simple? Beware complicated spellings or anything too funky. Avoid initials, like TWR Construction, because they don't mean anything to customers and they're hard to remember. TRW? RWT?

Before you decide to use your own first or last name, remember that you're the first person customers will want to see if they have a problem. There may come a time when you don't want to be so closely associated with daily operations.

Create a Compelling Slogan

In their book, *Positioning*, Jack Trout and Al Ries recommend choosing a marketing strategy that "positions" your business in the minds of consumers, allowing it to cut through the clutter of the advertising barrage we experience constantly. How do you differentiate a common business, like a car dealership, from all the rest? There are only so many "positions" that might be worth occupying in the mind of a car buyer, such as the lowest price, best experience, or most convenient. Most other industries are limited too. We opted against price because few people believe those boasts. Customers also discredit claims about superior customer service, so we looked for a different way to talk about our special experience. We trademarked "your *un*dealership" in 2002 and continue to use that slogan today.

Beware of puffery, or when you brag about "The best pizza in town." With a slogan like that, your pies better be outrageously good. When advertising makes promises that your business can't deliver, customers won't come back—and repeat customers are critical to your success because they bring revenue with minimal advertising cost. Bravado marketing does not inspire confidence in potential customers. Your marketing messages make a pledge, so make sure your products and services can honor that commitment when customers appear.

Advertising pioneer Rosser Reeves coined the term "unique selling proposition" to describe the cluster of special benefits offered by your business that differentiate you from your competitors. You want a memorable slogan that communicates those special characteristics. Brainstorm the qualities that make your business unique. Think about your company's reality. Once you understand what you do better than other businesses, it will be easier to find a memorable way of saying it.

Examples for small or medium-sized businesses:

- Plumber: We're #1 in the #2 business.
- Realtor: Everything I touch turns to sold.
- Radiator shop: A clean place to take a leak.
- Furniture store: More nice, less price.
- Auto dealership: We have good carma.

If you have a good slogan, stick with it. Only through constant repetition will the meaning of a phrase permeate your business and make an impression in the minds of prospective customers. You might get bored and want to revise it, but you would surrender hard-won brand equity.

Marketing Methods

I divide the broad practice of marketing into four main channels to deliver your message to the public.

- Paid media—advertisers who disseminate your message for a fee, such as radio stations and internet banner display companies.
- Owned media—your own resources, including your website and customer list.
- Earned media—reporters, bloggers, and others who tell your story.
- Social media—internet networks of affiliated people such as Instagram, Facebook, and YouTube.

Paid Media

With paid media, you exert control: you decide what your message is, and you choose where and when it appears. Unfortunately, big bills show up, and prospects often ignore or won't believe your message. How much attention do you pay to advertising? Many people intentionally avoid it, opting to change the channel or turn the page.

In the early years after we opened in 1998, before most car shoppers migrated to the internet to research vehicles and dealerships, we tried to tell our story using the traditional mass media of newsprint, radio, and television advertising. We struggled for the following reasons:

They are very expensive (especially in a major media market), so there was no way for our relatively small local business to afford the frequency required for prospective customers to remember our ads. Even on our community radio station, a single thirty-second radio ad costs roughly fifty dollars. If you're selling oil changes, or lawn mowing, or whatever, you need to generate substantial incremental sales to pay for each advertisement.

We could barely see any action for all our time and money spent. Results are famously difficult to measure with these channels—how do you know if they're working at all? We were spending thousands of dollars, but not seeing any meaningful difference in the number of customers visiting our showroom.

The reasons for choosing Planet over another dealership were nuanced and subtle, and these traditional media didn't offer enough space or time to communicate our best attributes.

When we advertised prices or deals, we attracted customers who were challenging to serve because they weren't interested in our experience. Nor were they particularly loyal. When they needed the next car, they went looking everywhere for another bargain.

For these reasons and others, we haven't advertised in any of the traditional media for years. We spend most of our advertising dollars on the internet. Digital advertising works better for most small businesses nowadays because you can laser focus your ads to the people who are most likely to do business with you, which means you can acquire customers at a lower cost. Furthermore, you can gain more insight into how much money you spent per customer.

Many businesses enjoy some success with search engine marketing. These are ads that appear during a search related to your business, and you "pay per click." We use this form of advertising, but only for search terms that we've found attract people likely to be buying a vehicle. In our area, we pay over ten dollars for a single click on a Google ad with the word "Subaru" in it, so we want to avoid paying for someone looking to "set the clock on a 2018 Subaru Forester." We prefer specific phrases that match buyer intent such as "lease new Forester." Even better is when prospects find us organically, without paying for a click, which we'll discuss in the next section.

Google currently attracts the largest amount of advertising dollars in the United States, followed by Facebook. Each offers different benefits. Google's technology allows you to associate your paid message with very specific search *terms*. Facebook collects a creepy volume of data points on its users so you can focus your message on very specific groups of *people*, such as senior citizens who live in a particular suburb. A variety of other advertising platforms might make sense for you, depending on your business. Some authors, for example, promote their books with Amazon ads. YouTube is the world's second largest search engine after Google, and might help your business if your products or services work well on video.

In addition to advertising our inventory online, we spend small sums on other forms of paid advertising. For example, at our Jeep dealership, we supply every new Wrangler with a quality exterior spare tire cover that appeals to adventurous off-roaders. The writing is upside down and says, "If you can read this, roll me over."

Before you sign another advertising contract, make sure you understand how the message fits into your overall strategy. You can spend a fortune getting your name out there, but what exactly does that accomplish? Coke spends billions on general branding, in the hope you'll ask for their cola by name the next time you need to order a drink in a restaurant. But if you own a local plumbing business, how much do you want to spend trying to make your company a household name? You will probably get more phone calls if you can figure out a way to appear on the first page of Google's search results when someone types in "my toilet won't stop running," along with the name of your town.

Owned Media

These are the communication resources you control, including your website and your customer database for emailing existing customers. Most local businesses will see the greatest return on their investment of time, energy, and money in this category. For example, it's easier to motivate an existing customer to do business with you another time (farming) than it is to find a new one (hunting). If you have a good email list of existing customers, you can stay in touch with them easily and inexpensively. Signs and banners are a one-time expense compared to a billboard that you have to rent monthly.

Your most profitable owned medium is your website. With a little imagination and enough effort, you can generate sales at a modest cost. Not only do most people buy things directly online, they also start researching and selecting items they will buy from brick-and-mortar stores. Beyond the obvious basics, a good website showcases your products in an appealing way and tells the story about why someone should choose your business over another.

When we opened in 1998, the average car purchaser visited between four and five dealerships before buying. Many customers walked in just to get a brochure and promptly left. Now, average car shoppers visit fewer than two dealerships before they buy a car. People are narrowing their choices by doing research on the internet long before visiting the store, which makes it critical to reach them while they're still making up their minds.

Your website can attract prospects organically through search engines. Google, Bing, and other search engines earn their revenue by serving up results related to the entered terms while charging businesses to place ads associated with those listings. If you're willing to do the hard work of creating a webpage highly relevant to certain keywords, you can appear in thousands of Google search results without paying anything. Instead of writing big checks for search engine *marketing*, we designed our digital strategy around search engine *optimization*. We developed planetsubaru.com as a research site, so people investigating vehicles and dealerships will find lots of useful content there. And while they learn all about Subaru, they discover the benefits of doing business specifically with us. You can do the same with your business by creating useful content for your shoppers. People will find your website during the research phase right before they're ready to buy.

To differentiate planetsubaru.com from other sites, we infuse our pages with the same fun, offbeat personality that you feel when you walk in the door. For example, we place dogs in unexpected places (such as popping out of the trunk on product videos) and we feature every one of our team members in a clever "AutoBiography" profile.

Earned Media

You win earned media when you attract attention to your business through external platforms such as newspapers, blogs, review sites, or industry newsletters. Perhaps the biggest advantage of earned media is the credibility factor—you could spend a fortune trumpeting your company, but no amount of paid advertising can match the credibility of third-party authorities or happy customers praising your business. You don't have to write checks for earned media, but you will need to invest time and energy. Unlike paid advertising, you can't control what people share about you, but you can solicit people who might be willing to share their favorable opinions with others.

Nowadays, people still share their experiences directly with friends and family, but they increasingly use online review sites to broadcast their satisfaction or disappointment with a business. A surprisingly large number of our customers tell us they decided to drive past closer dealerships due to the volume of authentic praise published by our customers. Of course there will always be a few hotheads who don't appreciate your efforts to satisfy them. We sell a few thousand cars a year and service five times that amount. With that volume of human interaction, there will be times when we encounter a very unreasonable person or make a mistake that a customer elects not to forgive. To keep our star ratings high on various sites, we reach out directly to unsatisfied customers, and encourage our happy customers to write reviews. We respond to every review.

We invite reporters to write stories when we have something newsworthy going on. We don't use a public relations firm—we just do it ourselves. Media outlets need fresh stories to report every day and they want some good news. Here are ways to do it:

Notify media when you do something special. For example, when we give a donation to an organization, we send a picture and media release to our local newspaper, and they usually publish it. We write the release in a straightforward way, just like journalists write, so they can publish our article with little or no editing.

Publicize the innovative things you do to help others. In journalism, the phrase "man bites dog" illustrates the principle that infrequent events tend to be more newsworthy. We generated a little media interest when we donated over $20,000 to a local environmental organization (with the forgettable photo of the principals holding an oversized check). But when we rented goats to help us with our landscaping, a variety of local and even national news outlets picked up that story. Both were stories about the environment, but goats mowing a lawn was more unexpected than just another donation.

Be alert to newsworthy events that appear organically, and make the most of them. During a heavy snowstorm, our flat roof started to sag, and we had to evacuate the building. That was the one and only time in our history that we were able to get a big-city television crew to broadcast our name on the six o'clock news. In another example, a dealer friend of mine, who lost a few cars to an overnight robbery, created a memorable segment when he told the reporter, on camera, "I don't know why they took the risk of stealing the cars at night, because our prices are so low we practically give them away during the day!"

Stories run only once, but they can live forever on your website if you gather and post them like we do on our News Stories page. Because people trust third-parties much more than commercial messages, these reports give credibility to the rest of our content.

Your odds of success increase with the volume of projects you undertake. We've placed stories about the solar panel array we installed on the roof, our partnership with a local school to plant and harvest fruit trees on our property, our unique hiring practices, and more. Some attracted more attention than others, because there is a luck factor in succeeding with earned media. Like viral internet stories, it's hard to predict what will blow up.

After a reporter writes a story, follow up with a thank you note. Stay in touch so reporters think of you when they need a quote about news in your industry. Respond quickly when they call to help them meet their tight deadlines.

Social Media

Social media channels are a hybrid of owned media and earned media. You control your page and shape the content, but you live by the policies and algorithms of social media companies. The more your followers share your posts, the more attention you'll get.

Social media are cheap, easy, and fun to manage. Your posts will maintain top-of-mind awareness with existing customers and make your company brand appealing and relatable. Most companies don't even need a separate team member to manage them.

Use caution when estimating the ability of social media to drive revenue-producing action by customers. Facebook, Instagram, Pinterest, and others support your marketing efforts, but are hardly a comprehensive marketing strategy on their own. Motivating existing customers to become followers or reaching new customers usually requires paid advertising to boost your posts. And most people use search engines, not social media, when they're preparing to spend money on a product or service.

Profit Wise Questions

- Can you articulate your overall marketing strategy? Do the people in your company responsible for advertising know what that strategy is?

- When was the last time you evaluated your media efforts to compare their costs to the results? How do you measure the success of a particular marketing method?

- Do you have a good understanding of who the customers are that you want to reach with your marketing?

- What do your team members think of your company's marketing?

- Are you communicating effectively with the people most likely to do business with you again (your previous and existing customers)?

- Are your marketing messages consistent with your company values?

Online Resources

This book comes with a sample media release and a marketing check-up worksheet to ensure you earn the highest return from your advertising investments. Find them at jeffmorrill.com/reader-tools.

CHAPTER 6

Quality Customer Service

Customers expect so much today because some businesses spoil them like never before. From Amazon Prime's same-day delivery to Zappos's generous return policy, people expect a great experience at a reasonable price. I recently called an 800 number after my chainsaw failed. I connected easily with a real person who shipped me a new saw with no questions asked (other than some diagnostic inquiries to confirm it wasn't an operator error). She didn't even ask me to return the first one. Experiences like these set high expectations that customers now bring with them to your business.

Even as the bar continues to be raised, superior customer service remains a profitable way to differentiate yourself from the competition, because much of the competition still can't put all the pieces together. We all still meet salespeople who can't execute the basics of a polite introduction or follow through on their promises. And we all still spend too much time on hold, waiting for agents who aren't friendly, empowered, or helpful. You will earn new business and future loyalty when your team executes customer service and sales activities with excellence.

Developing Sales and Customer Service Skills

Whether you're working with customers before they buy (sales) or after (customer service), your business is really just helping them meet their needs with your products. Sales and customer service are not exactly the same thing, but I combine them in this chapter because they require almost all of the same talents. Your team members need to make friendly connections with customers, solve problems, ask questions, and listen carefully. (Negotiation skills that might be necessary in some kinds of sales are explored in the next chapter.) Sales and customer service are also connected by a virtuous cycle: excellent customer service will motivate customers to return and buy from you again in the future. To delight our customers, we train our team members to do the following things:

Sincerely build rapport. When people are looking to buy a costly item, or they have a problem that needs a solution, they generally feel skeptical and anxious. They relax a little with a proper introduction and a brief conversation about normal things. Even under the best of circumstances, sometimes things go wrong, such as the delayed arrival of an item, so a good relationship can ease tensions that might arise. Also, spending a little time with customers before getting down to business helps you understand their personalities. For example, antsy and impatient people will prefer a speedy, efficient process. Others are slow and cautious and would feel rushed at that pace. To build rapport, we train our team to offer sincere compliments and ask questions to discover things they have in common. Pleasant, authentic conversations build connections and start relationships off on the right foot.

Remove obstacles. In sales, it's hard to escape the word "closing," as in, "the Realtor closed the sale today." But I never cared for the term, because it implies that the salesperson accomplishes the sale. It's the customer's money and the customer's decision, so a sale depends on a successful collaboration between the salesperson and the customer. The sales event is not so much a *closing* as it is an *opening* to a new long-term relationship between buyer and seller.

What do you do when a customer is interested, but not buying? Sales trainers typically teach salespeople to "overcome objections," but that sounds pretty forceful and unfriendly.

Instead, we think about removing obstacles that stand in the way of the customer's purchase. We're in a cooperative partnership with our customers and we're trying to meet their needs. Maybe a couple can't afford the vehicle they came in to see; we help them find something that does fit their budget. Or maybe customers can't make a decision today; we need to follow up in a professional way so we're the obvious solution when they are ready.

Don't be a smooth talker, be a smooth listener. The better you understand customers' requirements, the better you can serve them. Experts ask varied questions to assess wants and needs, and then they stop talking long enough to listen carefully to the answers. Those who are interested in others provide better service than those who try to be interesting.

Use questions to invite people to see things in a new way. As a naive young man, I thought that I could convince people by showing them the facts. I won arguments, but lost as many sales. Those failures helped me learn that most people resist direct persuasion. They prefer to discover things on their own. How do you help them do that? Ask them questions that focus their attention on things you would like them to know. Here's an example: leasing is not the best financing option for everyone, but it's great for people who regularly trade their cars before they pay off their loans. Instead of lecturing these customers on the merits of leasing, I learned to ask them questions, which allows them to learn at their pace and maintain a sense of control.

"Leasing is an alternative financing option that would lower your payment. It's ideal for your situation. Would you like to see the comparison?"

Okay, I guess. I've never leased a car, but I don't like the fact that I'll never own it.

"Do you own your car now?"

Sort of. I don't have the title because the bank keeps it until I pay off the loan.

"Did you know leases are like that too? Most people turn them in on the contracted maturity date, usually three years, but you can trade it in or pay it off at any time. Does that affect your thinking?"

So, it's basically just a different kind of loan?

"Yes. Would you like to learn more?"

To save $100 a month, I probably owe it to myself to at least consider it . . .

If you want people to look at something in a different way, help them chart their own course to the discovery. This showroom epiphany forever changed the way I interact with people. Even in my personal relationships, when someone is upset, I turn to questions: why do you feel that way, what do you think I did wrong, how can I make this right, are you willing to look at this from another perspective? First understand, then you'll be understood.

Helping Dissatisfied Customers

You need a process to manage customers who do not enjoy their experiences with your business and require immediate attention. Here are some tips:

Assign the proper team members to work with upset customers. You may or may not be the best person to solve customer problems. It can be challenging for owners who have invested so much in their businesses to hear some of the crazy stuff that angry people can say. Whoever takes the calls or emails needs an even temperament, along with the experience and authority to implement rapid solutions.

Allow customers to speak first. They'll know they've been heard, and you'll learn about their concerns. Show empathy through your tone, body language, and attentive listening. Keep an open mind. Maybe they're unreasonable, maybe your team screwed up, or maybe both are true.

Apologize. Sincere apologies mend fences. If you erred, fall on your sword and describe how you actually feel about failing to live up to your own expectations and theirs. Even if your team and systems worked properly, you can apologize for falling short of your desire to offer every customer an experience that exceeds their expectations. Saying "I am sorry for your inconvenience" shows the customer you are empathetic without entirely accepting ownership of the responsibility. Remember the old maxim that people don't care how much you know until they know how much you care.

Assure them you will help and make a plan. Don't overpromise, but don't underpromise, either. Upset customers want to know that someone will help them. Instead of guessing how to solve the problem, ask what they would like to see as a solution. "What would you like me to do?" If they can't move beyond the outrage of your mistake, guide the discussion toward things that can actually be done to resolve the situation. "We can't change what happened in the past, but we can make good decisions together now about how to make this right. How would you like to move forward?"

Solve the problem quickly, if possible. Each passing hour or day makes the problem worse. Delays intensify the negative emotions customers feel.

Stay in touch. If you can't solve the problem immediately, provide regular phone or email updates so they don't have to track you down. "I need to talk to the factory, and it could take me several days to reach someone and get a response. Just so you know I'm on top of it, I will call you this Friday with an update even if I haven't heard back from them." Then make sure you call them as promised. If they feel like they need to call you for updates, they won't have much confidence that you're taking the situation seriously.

It's okay to be firm. You don't have to take abuse or be bullied. When people use profanity or pass into an emotional zone where they can't listen or reason, you can ask them to change their approach or call back when they're in a better frame of mind. "I can see you're very upset. I'm a person, with feelings, and I need you to speak to me in a professional manner. If you're not able to do that now, let's schedule a time to do that after you've had a while to think about a good resolution."

The customer is not always right. If you've done all you can and the situation simply can't be resolved, advise them gently. If you need to ask them to leave, do it politely. Challenging them or pricking their egos may encourage them to continue the battle (often with lawyers), rather than just going away in search of a better experience elsewhere. Whenever possible, let them conclude calls or walk out on their own accord so they retain the feeling of control. "We've been on the phone for an hour, and now you're repeating what you told me earlier when I was listening carefully. Are we ready to conclude the call?"

Balance the ledger. When you solve the problem, determine whether you should do something extra to compensate customers, especially if your team dropped the ball. For example, when we damage a vehicle and need to send it to the body shop, we might perform a full interior and exterior reconditioning before returning the car, or give the customer a gift certificate for a future visit.

Learn from the event. At the end, ask your team how to prevent a repeat. Was it just a one-off fluke, or does a process or team member need attention?

Sales and Customer Service Strategy

Execute operational excellence. In any business, things will go wrong, and a simple mistake can turn what would have been a positive customer experience into a mediocre or negative one. To maximize the potential for smooth customer service and sales experiences, we focus on operational excellence, the classic management principle of gaining a competitive advantage by delivering higher levels of quality to customers. All else equal, we prefer to offer a smaller number of amenities and programs that we can master, rather than complex systems that increase the likelihood of a failure.

For example, some dealerships build cafés right into their service lounges, which sounds inviting until you consider how much effort it takes to run a restaurant, even a small one. The time, energy, and investment consumed by an in-store hospitality business won't be available to fix customers' cars right the first time, which is the whole reason they showed up in the first place. Before you pursue ancillary services, you need to consistently master the fundamentals of your core business operations.

We have created clear systems and processes in the form of Standard Operating Procedures (SOP). This way, we have one right way to do something so we can streamline it. Everybody who performs that task knows exactly what to do and how to do it. For example, to track the reams of paperwork necessary to transact a vehicle sale, we use a checklist just like pilots or surgeons do for their complex operations. To avoid smothering ourselves with our own red tape, we set a high bar for adding new policies, procedures, or processes. Each introduces another point of potential failure and requires costly planning, training, and management. If you focus on doing the few things that matter the most and avoid unnecessary complexity, your business will deliver more consistent results with fewer headaches.

Learn from your competitors at their expense. You don't need to be on the leading edge of everything, or reinvent every aspect of your industry. We do our share of experimentation and innovation—we landscape with goats, after all. But how revolutionary does an oil change need to be?

If you read enough business books, you'll begin to think that the first movers, the companies that sprint into a market to establish brand recognition and a customer base before others, somehow capture all the opportunity. But don't underestimate the power of letting other companies make the rookie mistakes so you can learn and improve on their expensive failures. Many leading companies in their industries were not first-to-market. For example, Myspace arrived way ahead of Facebook, and we know how that turned out. Companies that offer the most value to customers will rise to the top. Focus on doing what you do well, and hedge your bets by monitoring your competitors closely.

Seek the customers you want and surrender the others. Design your sales and service strategies and processes around the needs of the majority of your customers. Occasionally, we still get an old-school shopper who insists on a large discount from our already-low advertised prices. When this happens, we wish our prices started higher so we could oblige the customer with a big deduction. Sometimes we lose those sales. But that's okay, because we gain more than we lose by selling in a manner that appeals to the large majority of customers who prefer a more straightforward buying experience. In fact, in data gathered by Subaru of America, Planet sells roughly double the number of new Subarus expected of a store our size. Customers routinely drive past other dealerships to experience our unique model, even as we lose a few customers who prefer adversarial negotiation.

Reduce friendly fire. As they say in the military, "friendly fire ain't friendly." The expression describes situations where your own troops are mistakenly shooting their weapons at you, and their bullets are just as lethal as the enemy's. These self-inflicted wounds are caused not by external sources, such as unreasonable customers or product troubles, but by your own human error or system failure. Look for any patterns of mistakes and make corrections to your processes, training, or equipment to avoid repeating them. Do not tolerate repetitive problems. As author Paulo Coelho put it, "A mistake repeated more than once is a decision."

Create an environment where customers feel comfortable. For example, we have canine greeters. My brother started the tradition when we opened by bringing in his whippet and Italian greyhound to lie about the showroom and charm visitors. We currently have several dogs on duty, owned by team members who appreciate the opportunity to bring them to work. The dogs immediately put people at ease. Of all our team members recognized in customer surveys and online reviews, the dogs win the highest and most frequent praise!

Profit Wise Questions

- If I'm a customer with a problem that needs attention, what happens when I call or email your business? Who responds? How quickly? Are they empowered and organized enough to solve my problem?

- Are you recruiting, training, and retaining professionals who are authentic, friendly, motivated, and conscientious? Can they ask good questions, listen to the answers, and remove obstacles by solving problems?

- Are your sales and customer service processes easy to use for your team and customers?

- When an error occurs, how does your team discover the root cause and solve the problem to reduce reoccurrences?

- Are your customer experiences memorable and enjoyable enough that they will want to return and recommend your business to family and friends?

Online Resources

This book comes with a worksheet to help you build rapport. Find it at jeffmorrill.com/reader-tools.

CHAPTER 7

Negotiating

Some shy away from negotiating because reconciling different needs among people can arouse anxiety and other uncomfortable feelings. Some withdraw, and others become too focused on being right or proving a point instead of actually solving the problem. Even when negotiating with people you know and trust, like working out daily differences with family members, emotions can run high. Expert negotiators stay focused and centered.

To increase the likelihood that a negotiation results in a good outcome for all the parties, carefully choose the people you negotiate with. While you can't entirely avoid the need to work out differences with difficult people, you can go out of your way to do most of your business with people who have good character.

It also helps to bring the right attitude to the table. I prefer to think of negotiating in practical, cooperative terms. Most negotiations don't look anything like the adversarial, high-stakes conference room sessions you see on television, with the parties lined up on each side of a mahogany slab. I have participated in a few of those, but most routine negotiations are low-drama affairs: just a few people emailing or talking on the phone, trying to find a price and terms that make sense. When parties communicate functionally about their needs, they can get enough of what they want, and everybody can feel satisfied with the agreement.

The first thing to understand about negotiating is leverage. Leverage is just another word for power: the ability to confer benefits or impose costs on the other party. A mugger with a gun in a dark alley has significant leverage because your wallet is worth much less to you than your life. In most negotiations, though, neither party has an overwhelming advantage in leverage. If a customer doesn't like the price of our Outback or the quality of the service, she can try another Subaru dealership or look for another model at a Toyota dealership. If a customer is unwilling to pay a reasonable price for a car, or is treating our people rudely, we can pass on that transaction.

Leverage takes a variety of forms, including the ability to walk away from a deal or a relationship. Roger Fisher and William Ury coined the acronym BATNA in their book *Getting to Yes: Negotiating Without Giving In.* It stands for Best Alternative to a Negotiated Agreement. In a mugging, your BATNA might be fighting it out—not an appealing option considering the risks. But if you're trying to buy a business, perhaps there's another similar business for sale in the area that might fit your needs if the first seller can't meet your terms. Knowing your BATNA before you get too deep into a negotiation will help you avoid committing to undesirable deals.

To avoid giving away leverage, negotiators should disclose information to the other party with caution. Some facts in a situation are plainly visible—for example, if you make an offer on a house, then you're obviously very interested in owning it. But it isn't obvious to the seller that you'd be willing to offer an additional $20,000 because you've been looking around this neighborhood for the last two years, and this is the first house that meets all your needs. You might end up paying more than necessary if the sellers know how badly you want their house. I won't lie during a negotiation, but that doesn't mean I'm obligated to share every piece of information I have.

Let me stress that you should always negotiate ethically and responsibly. Throughout your business career, you will enter into negotiations with people of all different means, so don't abuse people with your skills. When it comes to negotiating with large businesses, such as the huge national banks that offer us loans, I drive a pretty hard bargain. I include multiple companies in my comparison so I know we're finding the best overall deal. We pay hundreds of thousands of dollars per year in interest on our loans; whatever margin I can shave off might be significant to me, but trivial to them. Unless we were to commit some kind of fraud, which of course we would never do, I can't think of a way we could ever take advantage of a national bank.

Compare that situation to our negotiations with Grant, who owns a small auto interior repair company. If we have a used car with a cut in the seat or a scratch on the console, he fixes it for us. Grant lives in the community and supports his family with the revenue he earns. We do not ask Grant for discounts because any savings would be insignificant for us, and might weaken his business. Just because you have leverage doesn't mean you should always use it.

Negotiation Tips

Prepare. I've been involved in negotiations where millions of dollars were at stake, and the other party had spent only the barest minimum of time coordinating amongst themselves, reading through the draft agreements, or asking about my needs. If something is important enough to negotiate, it's big enough to invest the time and effort to get organized. For most routine negotiations, modest due diligence will be sufficient. For example, before buying a new car, ask friends or look at reviews to find a reputable dealer, and look at your finances to determine your budget.

Ask lots of questions. It's easier to come to an agreement when you're clear on the other party's needs and objectives. You learn by asking and paying attention. There's a well-known exercise in MBA classes where the professor divides the students into two groups and asks them to divide a pile of oranges. The professor quietly tells one group to acquire the most peels, and the other group the most juice. The ensuing discussions reveal whether the negotiators can figure out how to get 100 percent of what they want, rather than just splitting the pile.

Practice empathy. Try to put yourself in the other party's shoes and imagine how you might achieve their objectives at less cost to you. F. Scott Fitzgerald said, "The test of a first-rate intelligence is the ability to hold two opposed ideas in the mind at the same time, and still retain the ability to function." Individuals may think through problems differently, but most of us share common human needs when negotiating: to feel a sense of control, to be liked and respected by others, and to be treated fairly and justly. You'll achieve more in negotiation when you can open your mind to varying perspectives.

Think in shades of grey rather than black and white. Speaking about relations among citizens who disagree with each other, the judge Billings Learned Hand spoke of the headspace you should occupy when trying to reconcile differences: "The spirit of liberty is the spirit that is not too sure that it is right." Things are not always as they appear, and no one has a monopoly on the truth. Perhaps you've heard the Buddhist parable about blind men encountering an elephant, each touching a different body part with its unique characteristics and failing to agree about the true nature of an elephant. We all tend to believe that our perceptions of the world are the one reality. Psychologists even have a term for this problematic phenomenon: naive realism. Remaining flexible in your thinking might help you identify creative solutions.

Pick your battles carefully. Reserve your disagreements for the issues that really matter, and let the rest go. If someone shares an opinion that you don't agree with during a negotiation, just move on. You win when you get an agreement that works well for everybody. It's not a debate and there's no panel picking the winner. Sometimes, as director Ken Burns says, "more than one truth can abide." Or as one of our salespeople used to say to bypass an inconsequential difference of opinion, "That's true too."

Don't be desperate to make a deal. You might make unnecessary and expensive concessions. We bought our dealership from two partners who had opened their business with more valor than discretion. They signed a lease that was too high for a start-up business and needed us to assume it until the end of the term. When John and I were negotiating, we required that they subsidize some of the rent for the first year, because we didn't want to fail the same way they did. They threatened to walk away, but John and I politely held firm. If that deal fell through, we could always pursue others. John and I were quite eager to own our first business, but we were also willing to wait for the right situation. The partners did eventually agree to that term because they needed someone to buy their distressed asset much more than John and I needed to own our first business.

Don't insult the other party. Don't drive such a hard bargain that you violate generally-accepted norms of negotiating protocol. Occasionally we have a customer (often reared in another culture where such behavior is more common) who will insist on a ridiculous initial discount, like $10,000 off. In the United States, such a gambit raises hackles. Humans cling tightly to their sense of justice and are willing to enforce norms even at some personal cost (such as the loss of a deal). Negotiating professionally and in good faith toward a mutually acceptable outcome is not a sign of weakness.

Focus on long-term relationships when possible. Consider whether you might be likely to negotiate with this party in the future. In a marriage, for instance, you don't necessarily want to demand too much because you'll need to work things out repeatedly through your years together. If you're selling your house, however, you're unlikely to negotiate with the purchasers ever again, so you might want to push a little harder (within your ethical limits). Even with one-off transactions, though, word gets around about how you conduct yourself. A reputation for indecent behavior could reduce the willingness of others to do business with you in the future.

Don't take things personally. Keep it cool and polite. Even if you don't approve of the other party's behavior, remember that negotiation is inherently stressful, and otherwise decent people may not have the same skills or experience to behave professionally. I've been involved with many customers who conducted themselves rudely during negotiations, but later became lifetime repeat purchasers. If you find yourself boiling over, step out, take a break, and regain your composure.

Remember that your leverage usually expires when you sign. Read contracts carefully before you sign them, because the terms of the deal are really set when the ink dries. We have found that vendors love to lock us into "evergreen" contracts that renew automatically every year. We were burned a few times, stuck with a company whose contract had recently renewed right before we decided we needed to end the relationship. Now, we simply require a clause allowing us out of the contract at any time with a thirty-day notice. It took me a long time to learn that almost everything in life is negotiable, especially as the value or stakes of a transaction increase. Your leverage is never as strong as before you sign, so ask for what you need before you complete a deal.

Negotiating the Price of an Item

Don't give something away for nothing. Negotiators make concessions to induce the other party into agreement. So, if you need to concede something that has value, make sure you get something in return. Imagine a couple asking me for a $300 discount on a car. In our early days, I would agree, thinking they would buy the car. But too often they thanked me for my time and left without buying. And then if they did come back, they would often ask me for yet another discount! I had made the mistake of giving a concession without asking for an order in return. I eventually learned to ask: "If I gave you that $300 discount, would you write an order with us today?" If the answer was "yes," I would proceed, but if the answer was "no," then I would politely ask if we could postpone negotiations until they were ready to move forward with a purchase.

Don't offer to split the difference. If you're selling an item for $5,000 and the other party only wants to pay $4,000, don't offer to meet in the middle at $4,500. Making that suggestion telegraphs a willingness on your part to make a concession without gaining any commitment from the other party. When you offer to split the difference, the buyer may thank you for conceding $500 and then counteroffer to split the new difference. Instead of offering to split the difference, invite suggestions on how you might bridge the gap: "We're $1,000 apart. What would work for you to keep this negotiation moving forward?" Then, if they offer to split the difference and the price makes sense, you can accept.

Make several smaller concessions, rather than one big one. For example, if you're selling a home, the buyer will feel better about multiple price reductions over the course of the negotiation because it suggests flexibility and good faith. Plus, the buyer gets to experience the positive emotions associated with multiple wins. One large initial concession might unintentionally send the message that more large discounts will be available later.

Avoid creating remorse in the other party. Sweat a little bit (literally or figuratively) in negotiations to show how hard you're working to reach an agreement. Since people bring anxiety to negotiations, they often leave the negotiating table wondering whether or not they got a good deal. For example, if you just accept the buyers' first offer right away, they may later wonder if they "left money on the table" or didn't get the best deal. They might even call later to revisit the terms or cancel the deal entirely. You win when you help the other party feel like they won. Here are examples of phrases you might use sincerely at the end of a negotiation:

- "That's a much bigger discount than I would normally accept, but our customer acquisition costs are lower with repeat buyers like you, so I'm willing to pass those savings along to you."
- "Congratulations on negotiating very favorable terms for your party. I do this for a living and I never would have guessed that you didn't!"

Profit Wise Questions

- Are you a confident, effective negotiator? What are your strengths and weaknesses?
- Do you often negotiate too little and get less favorable terms than you deserve? Do you negotiate too much, taking advantage of smaller businesses or damaging your reputation?
- How comfortable are you in conflict situations? What happens to your emotions? Do they interfere with your ability to think clearly?

- How do you prepare for an important negotiation? Have you ever role-played before a big meeting, with you taking one side and a colleague the other?

- How do you define a successful negotiation? Does this definition serve you well?

CHAPTER 8

Making Decisions and Solving Problems

If one of our salespeople says the wrong thing to a customer and loses a sale, how can we prevent a reoccurrence without thoughtfully investigating the context and asking the right questions? Did we fail in hiring, training, or managing? Or was it just a minor human error, the kind that might afflict anybody struggling with a cranky customer at the end of a long day? In the last case, perhaps no correction is required at all, except maybe a big hug and a good night's sleep.

You can't find the right solution without thoroughly understanding the problem. Spend your time figuring out the right question to ask before trying to generate fixes. I learned this lesson early in my career with a cursed car that just wouldn't stay fixed. Despite several attempts, we couldn't eliminate an intermittent tailgate noise on a Volvo 850 wagon. The car would squeak like fingernails on a chalkboard when driving over certain bumps. We replaced hinges, adjusted weather stripping, tightened the struts, lubricated everything we could reach—but every time we delivered the car back to the customer, he would call me a few days later with the exasperating news that the squeak had returned.

Including all the little parts such as screws and fasteners, there might be a few hundred individual components in the rear end of a car, and no practical or cost-effective way to replace them all. Before we gave up and took the financial hit of buying the car back from the customer, I invited Volvo's field service specialist to give us a hand. Serendipitously, Johan was an acoustical engineer, a grey-haired Swede who had helped design the 850. He took a look at the car, spun it around the block, and then wrote up a meticulous set of instructions for our technician. I was surprised that Johan didn't recommend replacing a single part. After tightening and adjusting the various components to Johan's standards, the squeak was gone, never to return. Johan told me something I still remember decades later: "Jeff, you asked, 'How do we stop all these parts from rubbing together?' But it's impossible to keep thousands of parts in a car from making contact. I asked instead, 'How can we move the frequency of the vibrations outside the range of human hearing?'" Johan came up with a better solution because he asked a better question.

We have a name for implementing reflexive solutions without first doing the hard work of examining causes: "command spasms." One day I walked into the shop and found the battery jump box chained to the wall with a lock. The service manager had grown frustrated with team members neglecting to return it after starting a car. Reactive cures might fix the original problem, but they often cause new issues that are even worse. Now everyone had to find him first, in our huge building, out on the lot, or in the bathroom! A few of us gathered to explore the problem. We couldn't figure out a practical way to address all the conditions that caused the box to disappear, including tow truck drivers borrowing it to remove cars.

Instead of asking how we could stop losing one jump box, we asked how we could ensure one was always available. And the answer to that question was easy: we bought five jump boxes— the best $500 we ever spent. Now, a box might disappear for a week, forgotten in a car, but it will typically find its way back when someone stumbles across it. And over the course of the year, we do lose a few forever, so we just buy a few more. In exchange for an infinitesimally small percentage of our annual revenue, we always have a jump box handy for anybody who needs one. Johan would be proud. The jump boxes continue to squeak, but no one can hear them.

Replace the command spasm with a quick, informal, improvised huddle of relevant team members. We usually don't require a scheduled meeting to solve problems. We have talent and experience, and a few minds usually suffice to work through a problem thoughtfully enough for a solution to emerge.

We used a huddle to solve the mystery of the disappearing hygiene products. We like to have our bathrooms generously stocked with things people might need in a pinch: baby changing stations with diapers and wipes, extra toilet paper, etc. A few years ago, our superintendent, Jonathan, asked why we needed to supply all those tampons and pads, almost one for every woman who used the customer bathroom. The small quantity of wrappers in the trash indicated that most were not used in the bathroom. I had always encouraged him to stuff the containers full, to reduce the risk of running out, but he observed that the higher the pile, the faster they disappeared. We convened a huddle of men and women. One of our salespeople suggested that maybe customers saw the bounty and took one for their handbags in case they needed it later, just like your grandmother purloined pink packets of Sweet'N Low from restaurants. If we put only a few in the basket, then women might feel like they were taking one from another woman who really needed it, rather than from the dealership, which they knew would just buy more. And sure enough, when Jonathan reduced the number available, our hygiene product expenditures plummeted.

We all tend to look at solution sets as binary choices (yes or no, all or none) when many other possibilities exist with just a little imagination. We could have phrased the hygiene products dilemma as a choice between buying huge quantities or eliminating them, but that would have left us with a less desirable outcome. When you don't like your options, see if you can find a way to get more options.

Decide Relentlessly

Lean into the volume of decisions you need to make. As a business owner, you encounter one fork in the road after another. Hire this person or that one? Buy or lease the new equipment? Pay off the mortgage or conserve cash? You'll make your share of mistakes, but overall, a bias toward action will grow your business faster than procrastination. Over the course of a career, a prompt yes or no works better than a long, slow maybe.

Look at the data and facts, but don't get lost in reports. Rarely will you have all the details you'd like before making a decision. Obtaining supplementary information incurs costs in delays, lost team member time, or data purchases. The optimal moment to stop seeking additional knowledge is not usually obvious, but one way to know is by considering the likelihood that more information would significantly influence the decision. Sometimes more figures and opinions just complicate matters, leading to a less desirable outcome because of information overload.

Not deciding to decide is still a decision, and usually not a very good one. But sometimes the right decision is to do nothing. When all the options to move appear too risky, you might want to stay put. When these situations arise, just make sure you're making an intentional decision and not just delaying.

Adjust your investment of energy based on the reversibility and gravity of a situation. Amazon founder Jeff Bezos wrote the following:

> "Some decisions are consequential and irreversible or nearly irreversible—one-way doors—and these decisions must be made methodically, carefully, slowly, with great deliberation and consultation. If you walk through and don't like what you see on the other side, you can't get back to where you were before. We can

call these Type 1 decisions. But most decisions aren't like that—they are changeable, reversible—they're two-way doors. If you've made a suboptimal Type 2 decision, you don't have to live with the consequences for that long. You can reopen the door and go back through. Type 2 decisions can and should be made quickly by high judgment individuals or small groups."

Start-ups routinely outmaneuver established companies because they make faster decisions. People in large corporations typically see mistakes costing them more than missed opportunities; newer businesses see things in reverse. Decades ago, executive Ross Perot said about the culture at General Motors: "At GM the stress is not on getting results—on winning—but on bureaucracy, on conforming to the GM system. You get to the top of General Motors not by doing something, but by not making a mistake." I don't suggest shooting from the hip, especially on Type 1 decisions, but the sooner you make a decision, the sooner you can start gathering relevant data about the results. And if you don't like the results, you can correct your course. Making decisions is similar to firing artillery: you usually don't hit your target on the first shot. The trick is noticing where the first shot landed, and then adjusting the equipment on subsequent shots to "walk" the shells to the target.

Even though we live in a business culture that fetishizes metrics, be careful about relying too much on numerical data when making decisions. As the saying goes, you can drown in data but starve for wisdom. There's a big difference between information and insight. Remember sociologist William Bruce Cameron's warning: "Not everything that can be counted counts, and not everything that counts can be counted," especially when it comes to personnel decisions. For example, we have a long-tenured salesperson who does not sell as many cars as her colleagues. Qualitatively, though, she shines. Her customers love her, and they refer friends and family. She enthusiastically shares our values. She lights up the whole showroom with her sunny personality. Numbers don't always tell the whole story.

Getting Good Advice

Create and maintain a "personal board of directors" to help you with big decisions. First described by author Jim Collins, this is the small group of people in your life you can trust to guide you because they have a record of consistently making wise decisions. They have your best interests at heart. Who are these people in your life? You can usually identify them by the visible harvest of their good judgment over the years. My board includes a selection of loved ones, old friends, fellow business owners, and Planet managers—perhaps ten or twelve people. They listen to the challenges and opportunities I'm facing, and give me new perspectives to consider before I make big or difficult decisions. They've never gathered all together, they don't all know each other, and some of them probably don't even know they're on the board. I never make a major decision without talking to at least several of them, and for the most important decisions (like changing my business role from quarterback to coach), I talked to every one of them, at great length. We can counter our biases by relying on other people because our behavior patterns and mistakes are more obvious to them.

Working with Attorneys

It was not obvious to me early in my career, but when it comes to hiring attorneys, remember that they are salespeople too. In order to understand their role and that of so many others in a capitalist world, remember the advice from the movie All the President's Men: "Follow the money." In business, you need attorneys almost from the beginning, and you'll continue to need them for the occasional thorny situation or relief from the tyranny of petty bureaucrats. But understand this crucial truth about attorneys that I learned the hard way: they are in business to make money.

You're naturally skeptical with most salespeople. When you walk into a stereotypical car dealership, for example, you know the salesperson is going to try to sell you something. You understand that there might be an adversarial nature to the proceedings, so you're naturally on guard. However, your lawyers present themselves as your advocate, which might lead you to believe that your interests are the same as theirs. But note that most attorneys take sides in a dispute based not on what they believe, but rather who is paying them. And even when you are paying them, their financial motivations might be very different than yours.

The most ethical lawyers privilege your interests over their profits, but they collect fees no matter what. They win even when you lose—especially litigators, who benefit more financially the longer and uglier the lawsuit, while your bills and suffering pile up. By nature, most litigators seek to litigate, so beware the person with only a hammer who sees everything as a nail. Suing others should be your absolute last resort.

Know Thyself

When you find yourself feeling intense emotions, take time to cool off so you can think clearly before making any important decisions. Don't make big choices under stress, when the frontal lobes of your brain—the seat of your highest analytical function— are offline. Avoid making decisions when you feel too high or too low. When possible, sleep on Type 1 decisions so you can tap into your unconscious brain and start fresh and clear tomorrow.

While I don't get especially "hangry," I've learned not to undertake difficult mental projects when I'm hungry. Sometimes we forget that we are animals, not robots, so it makes sense that hunger levels would affect cognition. In *Thinking Fast and Slow*, Daniel Kahneman writes of a study that shows parole board members were significantly less likely to approve parole when they were hungry or fatigued—before lunch and at the end of the day. Other things can interfere with good decisions: time pressure, lack of sleep, anxiety, problems at home, and any other factors that significantly affect your emotional state.

We make our best decisions when the analytical parts of our brain work in concert with the emotional parts. Even though you shouldn't make decisions when flustered, you can't make good decisions without any feelings at all. Damage to the orbitofrontal cortex, a highly evolved part of the brain that processes emotions, can render us incapable of making good choices, because our emotions are critical to our ability to analyze situations. Just make sure emotions work for you, rather than against you.

When you make decisions, do you instinctively lean toward your heart or your head? For example, if you had to settle a dispute between two members of your team who weren't getting along, would you prioritize the feelings of the people involved, or would you settle it based on the facts? If you're the kind of person who leads from the heart, you might hesitate to get involved for fear of causing more stress. The person who leads from the head will feel more comfortable taking action after a rational calculation, but might not be sufficiently compassionate during the conversations. Some people blend the styles naturally, but if you fall on one end of this spectrum or the other, you can compensate. For example, my brother and I are complementary, like Kirk and Spock. John leads with his heart, I lead with my head. We rely on each other to work through complicated matters that involve feelings and facts.

Are you a maximizer or a satisficer? In *The Paradox of Choice*, psychologist Barry Schwartz distinguishes these two fundamentally different types of decision makers. Satisficers are satisfied with "good enough." When they find something that meets their standards, they choose and move on. Maximizers look for the very best solution, and even after searching thoroughly and analyzing all the options, they suspect that they might have been better off with one of the roads not taken. Maximizers, not surprisingly, are significantly more likely to be clinically depressed. If you have these tendencies, beware of overdoing the research. Don't obsess over relatively insignificant Type 2 decisions, such as the paint color in the break room. If you have satisficer tendencies, make sure you devote sufficient attention to important Type 1 decisions. For example, don't accept the first quote for a big equipment purchase just so you can check that task off your list; do your research to make sure you're getting the best terms.

Evaluating Mistakes

All mistakes are not created equal. One of my mentors, Don Beyer, Sr., founded his Volvo dealership in 1973. He was a retired army colonel and provost marshal at West Point. He insisted that the after-action report on a decision should focus on the information that was *available* or *could have been reasonably obtained* at the time a decision was made. Driving drunk wasn't a good decision simply because you miraculously made it home without an accident, any more than the decision to run out to the grocery store on a nice day should be criticized because someone drove through a red light and totaled your car. If you hired the wrong person because of a sloppy process, that mistake demands a more rigorous investigation than the unpredictable event of the person quitting to care for a family member.

When evaluating mistakes, distinguish between a lack of experience and a lack of execution. Did the technician botch the repair because she never received the proper training (experience deficit) or because she interrupted the procedure to take a phone call (execution deficit)? Understanding the difference will help you formulate better solutions when mistakes occur.

Don't overreact to the pain of a mistake. Mark Twain wrote, "We should be careful to get out of an experience only the wisdom that is in it—and stop there; lest we be like the cat that sits down on a hot stove-lid. She will never sit down on a hot stove-lid again—and that is well; but also she will never sit down on a cold one anymore."

Find the Silver Lining

If you're really hard on yourself about mistakes you've made in the past, here's a technique that has helped me get out of my own dog house. It's up to you how you decide to make sense of your memories. I've learned to make peace with my mistakes and adversities by mining those experiences for wisdom and compassion. Shakespeare penned these words for Hamlet: "For there is nothing either good or bad, but thinking makes it so."

Perhaps you've heard the ancient Taoist parable of the Chinese farmer. He forgets to lock his barn, and his work horse runs away. His neighbor says, "That's too bad." The farmer replies, "Maybe." A few days later, the horse comes back, and arrives with an extra horse. The neighbor says, "That's good." The farmer replies, "Maybe." The farmer gives the wild horse to his son, who breaks his leg training it. The neighbor says, "That's too bad." The farmer replies, "Maybe." Later, the army comes to the village conscripting soldiers for battle, and the son is spared from joining. The neighbor says, "That's good." The farmer replies, "Maybe."

The story could go on and on, just as events keep unfolding in our lives. Don't fool yourself into thinking that every mistake is bad and that every fortunate event is good. You won't know that until some time has passed, so put short-term events in context. Philosopher Soren Kierkegaard said, "Life can only be understood backwards; but it must be lived forwards."

Profit Wise Questions

- Do you have a speedy, functional method for making decisions with key team members?

- Recall the last three bad decisions you made. Why did each fail?

- What are the circumstances under which you make your best decisions? Your worst?

- Do you make decisions too slowly, too quickly, or just about right?

- Who is on your personal board of directors? Do you use their wisdom to the fullest?

Online Resources

This book comes with a worksheet to help you analyze mistakes and prevent repeat failures. Find it at jeffmorrill. com/reader-tools.

CHAPTER 9

Making the Most of Your Time

Commercial real estate agents use the term "highest and best use" to describe a property's greatest financial utility. A quarter acre used to build a gas station in Manhattan is probably not the most productive use of the land; it will generate far greater returns as a skyscraper leased out to hundreds of tenants. Your time is as limited as New York City real estate. You only have so much, and once it's all used, there's no way to get more. What is the highest and best use of your time? Are you spending hours doing activities that you could delegate to someone at a lower pay scale?

Your most important responsibilities are usually not the most fun, so beware using your time on things you most like to do instead of those that will produce the most value. I was always very particular about the arrangement of cars on the lot, for both aesthetic and practical reasons. I enjoyed getting outside for fresh air and accomplishing something besides pushing paper around my desk. But it really doesn't make sense for me, or a highly-paid sales manager, to be moving cars around. Better to have one of our entry-level drivers move the cars after receiving clear instructions. The point is pretty obvious, but how many of your daily tasks really maximize your "hourly rate?" Here are some more tips to ensure you use your time in effective service of your personal and professional goals.

Take your bullets early in the day. For years, I would arrive at work facing at least one unpalatable and unavoidable task. Maybe it was calling an upset customer, unhiring someone, or mediating some dispute between team members. I became very practiced at these things, but I never enjoyed them. I learned to jump on these situations early, while fresh and alert, to prevent small problems from metastasizing. Later, I could relax a little after the most difficult work was done.

Recognize the dysfunctional relationship between perfectionism and procrastination. Try to obey the philosopher Voltaire's instruction to avoid making "best" the enemy of "good enough." Some people won't ever begin necessary projects because they're waiting for every piece to be in place before acting. If you want to write a business plan, for example, it's more important that you start with a one-page outline than it is to finish reading three books on the topic.

Arrange your day so it aligns with your natural energy flow. I am keenest in the mid-morning, a little dull after lunch, and I rally late in the day before crashing after four or five in the afternoon. Many people fit this pattern, though you might be different. I try to avoid scheduling meetings in the morning, and instead use those hours to focus on detail work, such as writing important correspondence or reviewing reports. After lunch, with my blood flow moving away from my brain and toward my digestive system, I like to get up and stretch my legs, check in with the team, or meet customers. By mid-afternoon, I take my meetings when I'm a little more relaxed and creative. I clean up my inbox at the end of the day since most emails don't require peak output, and I leave feeling organized.

Know when to quit for the day. You obtain less from your tenth hour at the office than you do from your second or third. In economics, the law of diminishing returns dictates that increasing investments of any kind eventually begin to decline in utility. Your energy and brain power decrease as the day wears on. We are biological organisms, capable of only so much production in a day. Sometimes you should just be at home eating dinner with your family instead of pushing your mind and body beyond their capacities.

Leave some slack in your daily schedule. I learned to avoid overscheduling appointments in the day, especially back-to-back. When much of my day is already committed, I experience stress sitting in meetings as urgent events emerge and require my attention.

Beware the cost of interruptions to your productivity. Your time at work is cut up into shreds by all the people who need to interact with you. Author Brigid Schulte calls this "time confetti." Your instant availability might contribute to a functional team, but it leaves no substantial chunks of time for crucial tasks, such as planning or thinking. I learned to work on those things at my dining room table before heading into work, knowing that I could never really concentrate in our frenetic retail environment. If you're a phone addict, understand that switching back and forth between your important work and your devices compromises the quality of your concentration for some time after. If you can't turn off your phone, at least move it out of reach. Reward yourself at hourly intervals with a hit from your phone instead of checking it every few minutes. Protect your flow state.

You don't need to respond to every email, but you do need to respond to important emails. Some people see email as a scourge, a time sink that serves other people's priorities. You can certainly waste time on email, but it's also an efficient tool when you use it properly. You would never completely ignore a phone call from friends, customers, or your team, and these important people feel similarly and justifiably slighted when you don't respond to their emails. If you're a non-famous person and have more emails than you can handle, see the book *Getting Things Done* by David Allen, because you may have a bigger time-management issue. Remember that emails are almost never the best way to handle complicated matters or resolve disputes. Instead, know when to pick up the phone, organize a huddle, or schedule a meeting.

Bring the right attitude to your problems. For far too long, I saw everything that wasn't perfect at the dealership, or in my life, as a headache. Now I understand that all of life is solving problems. You wake up in the morning feeling hungry, so you eat. Someone quits, so you hire someone new. Your knee hurts before you go bed, so you take an aspirin. When you don't have any more problems, you're dead. And while you're alive, the sooner you accept that the process of fixing stuff is pretty much the whole shooting match, the better you'll serve others and enjoy your life.

Despite everything that might be imperfect in your life, try to have nostalgia for your present situation. In Japanese, the phrase "mono no aware" roughly translates to "empathy for ephemeral things," or a longing for whatever your life offers right now, even as it may vary from your dreams or desires. For every important or mundane thing you do, there will come a time when you will no longer be able to do it. Perhaps it's hugging a loved one, taking a hike, or dressing yourself. Life's chapters often slam closed unpredictably. Think about that the next time you find yourself resisting events and wishing your circumstances were other than they are, because soon enough they will be different, one way or another.

Bandwidth

Writer Steven Covey popularized a foursquare matrix based on the following quote from a speech given by Dwight D. Eisenhower: "I have two kinds of problems, the urgent and the important. The urgent are not important, and the important are never urgent." Here's an example of the chart:

	Urgent	Not Urgent
Important	Phone system conked out	Reviewing pay plans and salaries
	Upset customer	Monitoring ad costs/results
Not Important	Vendor stops by to show product	Checking social media
	Customer calls to shoot the breeze	Rearranging showroom furniture

Important/Urgent: These tasks will usually find you rather than the other way around. They naturally rise to the top of your inbox.

Important/Not Urgent: Ideally, you spend most of your time here: planning, organizing, and leading. Unfortunately, urgent matters constantly intrude on your day and compete for your attention. Also, many entrepreneurs suffer from short attention spans, so they resist the crucial but unexciting activities in this quadrant.

Not Important/Urgent: The more of these you can delegate or ignore, the better.

Not Important/Not Urgent: It can be tempting to spend half an hour by the water cooler talking about weekend plans. The first five minutes might actually have some team-building value, but spend the other twenty-five back in your office doing the stuff that really matters.

The Life Cycle of a Career

Business owners usually progress through three key stages, and I've experienced all of them.

My growing years began in college, continuing through my apprenticeship at Don Beyer Volvo and into my first years at Planet Subaru. I was acquiring skills, making important personal connections, learning from my frequent mistakes, and developing the ability to see patterns.

During the power years, I combined the energy level of my youth with the experience necessary to accomplish challenging projects. During this time, Planet expanded: greening our operations, growing our facility, innovating in marketing and community service, multiplying our revenue, and developing the quality and size of our team.

Now I find myself in the wisdom years. I'm working smarter, rather than harder. I'm no longer willing to put in the long hours or make so many sacrifices. With fewer years remaining in my life, I need to select projects more thoughtfully. One of my mentors, Don Beyer, Jr., told me that a key to growing older is not learning how to do more with less, but rather less with less. In other words, choose fewer ambitions, more carefully. Use your time and energy preciously since you don't have as much to waste.

I was reminded about how quickly a career passes by when we welcomed the first of what would become many team members born after we opened in 1998. They weren't even alive during our crucial early years. All those years went by fast. Since we can't bottle time or save it for later, the next best thing is to make the most of it as it arrives and departs. We can aspire to fit Ralph Waldo Emerson's description of the enviable person who "walks abreast with his days, and feels no shame . . . for he does not postpone his life, but lives already."

Profit Wise Questions

- What are you doing now that you really need to delegate? Why haven't you already delegated these things? What do you need to change so you can get them off your plate?

- Where are you in the life cycle of your career? Have you adapted your business role to the unique demands of your current stage?

- Do you spend most of your time in the urgent/important quadrant? If not, would a different work location for part of the day help to reduce distractions?

- Are you buried by all the inputs in your life, such as emails, texts, memos, or meetings? What changes can you make to manage these in a healthier way?

Online Resources

This book comes with a worksheet to help you improve your ability to delegate. Find it at jeffmorrill.com/reader-tools.

CHAPTER 10

Success For the Long Term

One day in 2018, at age forty-six, just shy of Planet Subaru's twentieth anniversary, I cleaned out my office, passed along my dealer license plate to Dale, and got a ride home. The next day I left with Julie and our two cats to move to a new house in the woods outside Charlottesville, Virginia. My days as a player on the field had ended. It was time to become a coach.

Julie and I had been planning this for some time. I was fulfilling a promise that we would eventually move back to Virginia, and I knew I could not continue to show up at a car dealership for the rest of my life. The constant grinding had reduced a once mighty sword to a small knife.

Back in 1998, my brother and I were willing to take risks and work seven days a week, but we wanted to build a business where eventually our team and capital would do the heavy lifting. I had heard the family stories about my grandfather's experience owning a clam shack for almost twenty years, depending entirely on titanic effort for a competitive advantage. Eventually his family, body, and spirit collapsed under that strain. Long hours are necessary during the start-up phase, but business is a marathon, not a sprint, so you need to ease off once your business is established.

How to Avoid Running Out of Gas

Burnout is the chronic condition that occurs when your challenges take more energy from you than they return. You eventually lose interest in solving the same problems over and over.

The experience of burning out can be similar to going broke. In Ernest Hemingway's novel *The Sun Also Rises*, a character is asked how he went bankrupt. "Two ways," he answers. "Gradually, then suddenly." In my case, I had been pushing myself so hard for so long, that I didn't really notice the profound levels of accumulating exhaustion. Then one day I arrived at the dealership, turned my car off, and couldn't walk in the door. I had conducted enough interviews to replace departing team members, kept my cool enough times with irrational people, and suffered enough operational headaches. I just couldn't do it anymore. Fortunately for you, there are some things you can do to avoid, or at least delay, burning out.

Like they say on the plane, put on your own oxygen mask before assisting others. Your physical and emotional health are your greatest assets. You can't honor your responsibilities to others if you're sick, depressed, exhausted, or addicted. Eat well, exercise routinely, see your doctor, and beware using alcohol or drugs to numb the pain.

Set boundaries with your schedule. Looking back, I put in too many hours at the dealership for too many years, not realizing I was depleting my physical and emotional reserves. I was asking too much of my body and spirit. I should have paced myself better. I could have delegated more, worked fewer weekends after the start-up phase, and taken more vacations.

Stress out in proportion to the severity of the situation. Concentrate on things that really matter, and let go of things that don't. For example, I used to push our messy salespeople to keep their desks tidy because the showroom is our theatre, and we are on stage. Customers consciously or unconsciously form opinions about our competence based on the appearance of our workspace. I still believe this as passionately as I ever did, but I stopped nagging salespeople about their desks. There are only so many priorities a company can focus on, and

I've learned to fight the battles that matter more. Psychologist Williams James counseled, "The art of being wise is knowing what to overlook."

Beware the defects of your virtues. Too much medicine can become poison. For years, I thrived by out-working and out-suffering the competition. But the problem with building success around the ability to endure pain is that the pain just keeps coming! How long can anyone do that without paying a high mental or physical price? Be good to yourself. If you're a workhorse, know when to take a break. If you're a perfectionist, learn how to accept good enough.

Try to find at least one thing you can enjoy at work every day. Don't postpone joy or suffer too much in the vain hope that someday you can rest on your achievements, a situation Warren Buffett compared to "saving up sex for old age." Entrepreneurs usually make profound sacrifices and expose themselves to serious risks in pursuit of wealth. Even if they eventually succeed, they discover that the pot of gold under the rainbow does not bring all the pleasure they expected. Psychologist Tal Ben-Shahar called this illusion the arrival fallacy. Deferred gratification has its benefits, but experience your present days for what they offer, too. When we were kids and came home thirsty after playing outside, my mother would stop us from pouring a tall glass of orange juice: "Juice is expensive! Drink a glass of water to quench your thirst, and then you can enjoy the juice." She insisted we "swish it around," which is now our family shorthand for making sure we savor the moment. Find something worth swishing around every day.

Make time for friends, especially if you're a guy. Women seem to naturally invest more in their network of friends, even if they generally have less free time than men. Most of my male peers allocate their time and energy to only three things, in this order: work, parenting, and marriage. They allocate little time for anything else, so they miss out on friendships. Good friends provide a unique form of sustenance, so choose them well. I'm not sure you're exactly "the average of the five people you spend the most time with," as entrepreneur John Rohn asserts, but people definitely rub off on each other. Spend time with those you admire and you might become more like them.

Groom your own successor, and help your key managers do the same. You'll be ready for an event that might quickly remove one or more of you from action. Mentoring takes years, so the earlier you identify and develop these key players, the better. My operational successor, Dale, joined us as a salesperson in 2002. We promoted him repeatedly as he grew his skills, and we continuously gave him other opportunities that would expand his network and perspectives, such as including him in important meetings. He would later become a partner. When the time came for me to leave the building, he was ready. We have solid managers in each of the dealership's four departments (sales, service, parts, and accounting) who have been with us for years. Each one mentors an assistant manager. The managers enjoy the benefits of a competent sidekick, and the assistant managers develop new skills.

Know when to step back. For their health and the health of their companies, most founders eventually turn over the operational reins to a seasoned executive. Prominent examples include Facebook's Mark Zuckerberg (Sheryl Sandberg) and Apple's Steve Jobs (Tim Cook). It's not easy to let go. A Chinese proverb says, "The hard part about riding a tiger is getting off." I decided it was my time when I lost the thrill of trying new things and saw that I was no longer mustering the high level of professional enthusiasm that our team deserved.

Set Your Intentions

It's up to you whether you want to spend your life making excuses about why you can't make progress toward your dreams, or whether you want to take responsibility for making them happen. You are the biggest obstacle to success in your life. Luck does play a huge part, but I've seen privileged people squander their good fortune, and I've seen a few people beat long odds to make winning hands out of crappy cards. Until we create a society with greater equality of opportunity, some people will have a much smoother path to success than others. But whatever station you occupy in life, you can make decisions that will move you closer to your ambitions. That means making changes. As author Derek Sivers says, "I usually get where I'm going by leaving where I've been."

No matter how hard you work, you will probably never become a Warren Buffett or a Michael Jordan—their achievements required an almost impossibly rare alchemy of talent, luck, and effort. But you can improve your financial condition or get into physical shape. Start by moving past your own limiting beliefs, what poet William Blake called "mind-forged manacles."

The most accomplished people I know hold themselves accountable to some kind of annual, written plan. They know that setting a goal is the equivalent of aiming a gun before firing it. You might accidentally hit a target using the spray-and-pray method, but it's not a good bet. Some people spend more time planning a vacation than they do their life, with predictable results. Don't leave the most important things in your life to chance.

I started writing down my aspirations in 1994. I used to call them goals, and some were extremely ambitious, including serving as the Governor of Virginia someday. I struck out on that one and many others, but hit a few home runs, including the founding of Planet Subaru. As I've satisfied some of my younger desires to ascend various summits, I'm now more interested in broader pursuits, such as improving myself as a person and increasing my ability to serve others. I began referring to my goals as intentions, thinking of them as lifelong projects, rather than tasks to check off.

Without suggesting it's easy, there's nothing especially complicated about changing your life. You just need to adjust what you do today and keep doing it. Author Brian Tracy said, "Successful people are simply those with successful habits." Think about brushing your teeth, something you do twice a day with little thought or willpower because the habit drives your behavior. You made it part of your daily routine and you just do it.

I recommend a straightforward process to develop your intentions. First, you need to find the gap between your current and desired circumstances. If the changes you want to make in your life are not immediately obvious to you, start with a piece of paper and write some brief responses to these questions. If you're more extroverted, explore aloud with a confidant:

- What are my "first principles" or fundamental life values that drive my decisions?
- Where did I learn these values? Why are they important to me?
- What do I want more of in my life?
- What do I want to get rid of or avoid in my life?
- What dreams do I want to pursue?
- How am I hurting people I care about?
- What would I like to be said about me at my funeral?
- What are others doing to get the results I would like to see in my life?

Additional Steps:

After identifying your intentions, commit them to paper. As the proverb says, a short pencil is better than a long memory. Writing activates the subconscious parts of your mind that affect your decisions and behavior. Also, written goals make you accountable.

Limit the number of intentions to a handful so you can focus your energy and attention. In your first year, to walk before you run on the path to success, you might want to choose just a single intention. Succeeding with one might build your confidence in making changes and help you develop the meta-practice of positive habit formation.

For your more task-oriented goals, identify *specific* sub-goals and deadlines to get you there. If you want to begin enjoying the benefits of a plant-based diet, it might look something like this:

"Choose a diet that's healthier for me and the planet."

- Eat entirely vegetarian every Sunday.
- Order a book on vegetarian nutrition within thirty days.
- Finish it within sixty days.
- Take a vegetarian cooking class within ninety days.

Share your intentions with your personal board of directors. I email mine to all the people in my life who care about my personal development. They support and encourage me, and they keep me accountable in an organic way by asking me about them when we see each other.

Review them from time to time so you don't lose focus. Before undertaking any meaningful project in your life, it can be overwhelming and discouraging to consider the scale and quantity of the tasks required. But don't underestimate the value of small steps, because they help you generate momentum, and the effects add up cumulatively. Our various businesses would grow into a huge enterprise, but that journey began when I picked up the phone and started inquiring about dealerships for sale. It was that one small step that led to the next one and the next one, until I had gone much further than I thought I could. What's one small step that could move you closer to a big aspiration?

Profit Wise Questions

- Does a typical workday give or take more energy than the job returns? Over time, do you feel like you've lost any enthusiasm for your tasks and responsibilities?

- Do you generally have healthy boundaries between your work life and your personal life? What would your family members say?

- How many friends could you call late at night for help with a problem? Have you been a good friend?

- Are you grooming a successor? If not, do you have a plan to sustain your business if you're temporarily or permanently gone?

- Do you have any kind of intention-setting process? If not, do you have a good reason not to try it?

Online Resources

This book comes with a detailed worksheet to help you develop your intentions, and an actual example of my intentions from a few years ago. Find them at jeffmorrill.com/reader-tools.

Conclusion

I spent my prime years building wealth, and I'm very grateful that it worked out. But I discovered that having a whole lot of change in my pocket didn't really change my life a whole lot. Now I live in a nice house and have more free time, but I'm still me. Assuming you enjoy some reasonable level of financial security, other factors will affect your life experience much more than money. These include the quality of your intimate relationships, the satisfaction you obtain from your daily activities, and especially your health.

While you earn a living, remember that financial achievements constitute only a small part of a worthwhile life. Honorable businesses consider the needs of everyone who depends upon them, and they serve causes nobler than just the bottom line. Companies that harm people or the Earth in wanton pursuit of profit are little more than wrecking balls. The world as we know it will not long endure if short-term self-interest drives every decision.

As my father says about creating and sustaining a just society, we need institutions to function with "love in the model." My father was a teacher, and he devoted his professional life to growing knowledgeable, ethical citizens. When he speaks of incorporating love into the model, he means we should pursue our goals with empathy and compassion. Otherwise, what is all the achievement for?

Your life is a brief candle. Cast light where there is darkness, and share your flame with the world by living with love in your model.

About the Author

JEFF MORRILL co-founded Planet Subaru, "your *un*dealership" in 1998, and built it into one of the most successful privately-held car dealerships in the United States. He later started other businesses in automotive retail, real estate, telecommunications, and insurance that generate over $100 million in combined annual revenue. His achievements in building profitable and ethical companies have been featured in a variety of national media including *USA Today, Entrepreneur Magazine, Automotive News, The Boston Globe*, and others. Jeff lives with his wife, Julie, outside Charlottesville, Virginia, on a mountain he refers to as "The Morrill High Ground." Get in touch at jeffmorrill.com.

CONNECT WITH JEFF MORRILL

Sign up for Jeff's newsletter at
www.jeffmorrill.com/subscribe-for-free

To find out more information visit his website:
www.jeffmorrill.com

BOOK DISCOUNTS AND SPECIAL DEALS

Sign up for free to get discounts and special deals
on our bestselling books at
www.TCKpublishing.com/bookdeals

CPSIA information can be obtained
at www.ICGtesting.com
Printed in the USA
LVHW021634260921
698747LV00007B/1290